FAMILY MEALS

CHARMAINE SOLOMON

HAMLYN

Published 1993 by Hamlyn Australia
an imprint of Reed Books Australia
a division of Reed International Books Australia Pty Ltd
22 Salmon Street, Port Melbourne, Victoria 3207

Copyright © Charmaine Solomon 1993
Copyright © photographs Michael Cook 1993

All rights reserved.

Designed by Louise Lavarack
Photographs by Michael Cook
Styling by Margaret Alcock
Food cooked by Jill Pavey and Nina Harris
China: Apilco and Pillivuyt from The Bay Tree Kitchen Shop, Woollahra
NSW
Ceramic bowls: Made in Japan, Neutral Bay NSW
Typeset in 9½ on 12pt Berkeley Old Style Book by Midland Typesetters
Produced in Hong Kong by Mandarin Offset

National Library of Australia
  cataloguing-in-publication data:

Solomon, Charmaine.
  Family Meals

  Includes index.
  ISBN 0 947334 49 1

  1. Cookery, Oriental. I. Title. (Series: Asian cooking library).

641.595

INTRODUCTION

When parents like spicy food but children refuse to eat it, a restaurant situation develops in the home kitchen. Two servings of this, one of that . . . Before you know it, there's no such thing as a family meal.

While I would never advocate forcing food on children, if you want yours to have well-educated palates it doesn't hurt to expose them to all kinds of food. From a young age my children have eaten their way around the world without travelling further than the kitchen. As a consequence, they enjoyed a healthy curiosity about food and how to prepare it.

As a working mum, I depended on quickly cooked, stir-fried dishes as the mainstay of our week-day dinners: curries were a feature on weekends. The health aspects of this kind of food were also a consideration. Children will usually eat crisp, crunchy, half-raw vegetables, but will reject the same vegetables fully cooked. Nutrition is better when vegetables are stir-fried the Asian way.

Curries need not be hot. Many authentic curries employ no hot spices at all. Of course, there are people who love searing hot dishes, but of all the spices used, only one or two are pungent and stinging; the rest are fragrant and aromatic, making meals a sensory experience.

Young children and some adults cannot take the sting of chillies—nor should they have to. Keep the main dishes mildly spiced, so they won't be put off by tasting something with more fire than they were expecting. For those adults who are chilli addicts, provide a jar of chilli relish, a salad containing fresh chillies, or a bottle of chilli sambal.

This advice isn't something new I just thought up. It is the way extended families in Asia cope with catering for three or sometimes four generations from the same kitchen. My suggestions are classic dishes, exciting enough for adults but adapted for the enjoyment of the younger or much older age group.

May I suggest that, when eating an Indian meal, especially one that features flat breads, you eat with well-washed hands. That way, when the kids grow up and travel in Asia, they won't be caught flatfooted (or should I say flat-handed?). And when the meal is of the kind that would, in its country of origin, be eaten with chopsticks or with fingers—well, do just that. It's fun and is a skill that should be learned young.

Cooking and eating 'foreign' food is just one part of educating the family to be citizens of the world and the recipes in this book have been chosen so that everyone can look foward to family meals as an enjoyable experience.

SOUPS

Use this stock as a starting point for soups. To reduce fat content, chill stock until fat globules solidify on surface, then lift off. Add noodles and this stock makes a quick and tasty meal for children. Or make egg drop soup simply by pouring beaten egg into the boiling stock.

CHICKEN STOCK

- *2 kg (4 lb) chicken soup pieces*
- *3 L (12 cups) cold water*
- *1 teaspoon black peppercorns*
- *8 slices fresh ginger*
- *3 stalks celery, with leaves*
- *2 onions, peeled and halved*
- *few stalks fresh coriander, including roots*
- *salt to taste*

Put chicken pieces in a large saucepan. Add remaining ingredients and bring to boil. Cover and simmer for 1½ hours. Strain. Add salt to taste.

SOUP WITH MEATBALLS
Serves 4

- *375 g (12 oz) minced pork*
- *½ teaspoon finely grated fresh ginger*
- *1 clove garlic, crushed*
- *salt to taste*
- *2 tablespoons finely chopped spring onions*
- *2 slices soft white bread, crumbed*
- *1 egg yolk*
- *5 cups Chicken Stock (see p. 1)*
- *1 tablespoon dry sherry*
- *3 teaspoons cornflour*
- *1 teaspoon oriental sesame oil*
- *2 spring onions, sliced thinly*

Mix pork with ginger, garlic, salt, chopped spring onions, breadcrumbs and egg yolk. Form teaspoonfuls of mixture into balls. Bring stock to boil, drop in balls, cover and simmer for 10 minutes then remove with a slotted spoon.

Mix sherry with cornflour and 2 tablespoons cold water and add to simmering stock. Boil, stirring, for about 1 minute, or until soup is clear and slightly thickened. Stir in sesame oil. Return meatballs to soup and serve garnished with spring onions.

This soup is so named because of its 'short' dumplings or wontons.

SHORT SOUP
Serves 6

- 3 dried shiitake (Chinese) mushrooms
- 125 g (4 oz) raw prawns
- 125 g (4 oz) minced pork
- salt to taste
- 1 tablespoon light soy sauce
- 1 small clove garlic, crushed
- ¼ teaspoon finely grated fresh ginger
- 4 spring onions, finely chopped
- 125 g (4 oz) wonton wrappers
- 2 L (8 cups) Chicken Stock (see p. 1)
- 1 teaspoon oriental sesame oil

Soak mushrooms in hot water for 30 minutes. Squeeze dry, discard stems and finely chop caps. Shell and devein prawns. Chop finely. Combine mushrooms with prawns, pork, salt, soy sauce, garlic, ginger and half the spring onions.

Put a level teaspoon of mixture in centre of each wonton wrapper, moisten edges with water and fold diagonally to form triangle. Press edges to seal. Moisten 2 corners at base of triangle and join. Drop wontons into boiling stock and stir until it boils again. Simmer 10 minutes. Sprinkle with sesame oil and remaining spring onions.

COMBINATION LONG SOUP
Serves 4 to 6

- 8 dried shiitake (Chinese) mushrooms
- 2 eggs, beaten
- salt and pepper to taste
- few drops oriental sesame oil
- 250 g (8 oz) fine egg noodles
- 2 L Chicken Stock (see p. 1)
- 2 tablespoons peanut oil
- 2 cloves garlic, bruised
- 4 slices fresh ginger
- 250 g (8 oz) chicken fillets
- 250 g (8 oz) lean pork, shredded
- 1 cup sliced mustard cabbage or Chinese broccoli (gai larn)
- 2 cups sliced white Chinese cabbage
- 3 spring onions, chopped
- 2 tablespoons light soy sauce
- 1 teaspoon oriental sesame oil

Cover mushrooms with hot water and soak for 30 minutes. Cut caps into thin strips. Beat eggs with salt and pepper. Pour half into heated omelette pan lightly greased with sesame oil and make a thin omelette. Turn out and repeat with remainder of beaten egg. Roll up omelettes, slice thinly and reserve for garnish.

In a large saucepan of lightly salted boiling water cook noodles for 2 minutes. Drain. Rinse with cold water to separate strands, drain again. Bring Chicken Stock to boil in saucepan.

Heat peanut oil in a wok; add garlic and ginger and fry until brown. Discard. Stir-fry chicken and pork in flavoured oil over high heat until colour changes. Add vegetables and fry 2 minutes more. Add cooked meat, vegetables and noodles to hot Chicken Stock and when soup returns to boil, stir in soy sauce and sesame oil and serve immediately, garnished with reserved omelette strips.

MIXED MEAT AND VEGETABLE SOUP
Serves 6

- *4 dried shiitake (Chinese) mushrooms*
- *125 g (4 oz) chicken fillets*
- *2 stalks Chinese broccoli (gai larn)*
- *125 g (4 oz) barbecued pork or roast pork, diced*
- *2 tablespoons peanut oil*
- *½ teaspoon finely grated ginger*
- *½ teaspoon crushed garlic*
- *6 cups Chicken Stock (see p. 1)*
- *2 tablespoons dry sherry*
- *2 tablespoons oyster sauce*
- *2 tablespoons cornflour*

Soak mushrooms in hot water for 30 minutes. Discard stems and slice caps thinly.

Cut chicken into paper-thin slices, partially freezing meat first. Cut broccoli stems diagonally into thin slices.

Heat 1 tablespoon oil in wok, add ginger and garlic and stir for a few seconds, then add broccoli and toss over high heat until colour deepens. Remove to dish. Heat remaining oil and stir-fry chicken.

Bring Chicken Stock to boil. Add sherry, oyster sauce, chicken, broccoli, sliced mushrooms and pork. Mix cornflour with ¼ cup cold water and add to soup, stirring constantly, until soup is thickened and clear. Serve immediately.

Make sure the pumpkin you select is ripe—brightly coloured, with a firm texture and sweet flavour. Buy cut pumpkin if you're unsure, because what you see is what you get.

THAI PUMPKIN AND COCONUT SOUP
Serves 6

- 750 g (1½ lb) ripe pumpkin
- ½ cup dried shrimp
- ¾ cup chopped shallots or onions
- 2 stems lemon grass, tender white part only, finely chopped
- 1 cup canned coconut milk
- 1 tablespoon fish sauce
- lime juice to taste
- 1 cup Chicken Stock, optional (see p. 1)
- few fresh basil leaves

Peel and dice pumpkin. Soak dried shrimp in hot water for 10 minutes. Place drained shrimp with shallots and lemon grass (or finely peeled rind of 1 lemon) in blender or food processor and purée with a little water. Combine purée with ½ cup coconut milk and 1½ cups water and bring to boil, stirring constantly. Simmer for 5 minutes. Add pumpkin and simmer until pumpkin is tender. Stir in remaining coconut milk and bring back to boil. Add fish sauce and lime juice to taste. (If you prefer thinner soup add a little hot Chicken Stock.) Throw in basil leaves just before taking off the heat.

CHICKEN AND SWEETCORN SOUP
Serves 6

- *250 g (8 oz) chicken tenderloin or breast fillet*
- *½ teaspoon salt*
- *2 egg whites, beaten to a froth*
- *3 tablespoons cornflour*
- *6 cups Chicken Stock (see p. 1)*
- *1 tablespoon light soy sauce*
- *2 tablespoons dry sherry*
- *1 x 440 g (15 oz) can creamed corn*
- *1 teaspoon oriental sesame oil*
- *1 spring onion, finely sliced*
- *½ cup shredded ham*

Trim white sinew from chicken tenderloins and mince or chop so finely that the flesh is almost a purée. Add salt, 2 teaspoons cornflour and a tablespoon of cold water and mix well. Fold in egg whites.

Bring Chicken Stock to boil. Add remaining cornflour blended with ¼ cup cold water, stirring until stock returns to boil. Boil for 1 to 2 minutes until it thickens. Add soy sauce, sherry and creamed corn and stir. Add sesame oil and puréed chicken and stir gently as it simmers for 1 to 2 minutes. Serve garnished with spring onion slices and ham.

A South Indian soup with a pleasantly spicy flavour.

LENTIL MULLIGATAWNY
Serves 4 to 5

- 1 cup red lentils
- 1 clove garlic, chopped
- 1 small stick cinnamon
- 2 whole cloves
- 4 cardamom pods
- ¼ teaspoon black pepper
- 1 large onion
- 1 tablespoon ghee or oil
- 4 curry leaves
- salt to taste
- ½ teaspoon garam masala (see p. 73)
- ½ cup canned coconut milk (optional)

Wash lentils thoroughly. Drain. Place in saucepan with garlic, cinnamon, cloves, cardamom, pepper and half onion. Add 1.5 L of water, stir and bring to boil. Cover and simmer until lentils are soft. Strain and remove whole spices. Push lentils, onion and garlic through sieve, or lift out spices and purée mixture with hand-held blender in saucepan.

Finely slice remaining onion. Heat ghee or oil and fry onion and curry leaves, stirring frequently, until onion is brown. Add lentil purée, salt and garam masala. Simmer for 1 to 2 minutes or until heated through. If you prefer a richer soup, add coconut milk and stir until heated through.

RICE, NOODLES, BREAD

Rice, noodles and bread are staples of an Asian diet. Breads may be unleavened—known as rotis—or leavened, and baked, fried or steamed. At least one of these carbohydrate components features at every meal.

Rice is easy to cook when you know the rules. Noodles hardly need rules—just be sure not to overcook them. If you can cook pasta, use the same method, but be aware that some types of noodles will cook in as little as 1 or 2 minutes, so follow the directions in each recipe for that particular variety.

For Chinese or Japanese meals, use short grain rice like our Calrose variety—when cooked the grains will be well defined but still cling together which makes for easy eating with chopsticks. One cup of raw rice yields almost 3 cups cooked rice.

Long grain rice is preferred in other cuisines. For Indian meals, basmati rice is perfect with its thin grains and distinctive perfume. In Thai cooking or for general use, I like jasmine rice (another perfumed variety). As a rule, long grain rice cooks drier and fluffier.

Breads are a little more time-consuming—the dough has to be made, the mixture left to rest and then shaped or rolled out. But they are delicious, nutritious and well worth the time and effort. If you really don't have time, buy Middle Eastern flat bread from the supermarket or delicatessen and keep some on hand in the freezer. It's not quite the same, but certainly more in keeping with an Eastern meal than a sliced sandwich loaf!

This is the Chinese method of steaming rice. (If cooking long grain rice by this method, increase the amount of water to 3½ cups, as long grain rice has greater absorbency.) At the end of cooking time, fluff up rice with a fork. Always use a metal spoon to transfer rice to serving dish—a wooden spoon will mash the grains.

STEAMED WHITE RICE
Serves 4 to 6

- 2½ cups short or medium grain rice
- 3 cups water

Wash rice if necessary and drain well. Put rice and measured water into a saucepan and bring to boil over high heat. Boil rapidly for 1 minute, then reduce heat to medium and continue cooking until holes appear on surface of rice. Cover pan with tight fitting lid (or place a layer of foil between lid and pan), reduce heat to lowest setting and continue cooking for 10 minutes. Turn off heat and leave rice for further 10 minutes. Do not remove lid during this time.

For rice that is to be fried later, turn rice out onto a large tray immediately it is cooked and allow to cool quickly, then refrigerate until quite cold and firm.

Improvise on this theme by adding one or more of the following ingredients after frying briefly in oil: chopped ham, barbecued pork or bacon, prawns or peas.

SIMPLE FRIED RICE
Serves 4

- 2 tablespoons peanut oil
- 1 teaspoon finely grated fresh ginger
- ½ teaspoon crushed garlic
- 4 cups cold cooked white rice
- 2 tablespoons light soy sauce
- 6 spring onions, sliced diagonally

Heat oil in wok and on medium heat add ginger and garlic and stir-fry for a few seconds, then add rice and toss constantly until grains become separate and lightly coloured. Sprinkle with soy sauce and toss until evenly mixed. Add spring onions and toss over heat a minute longer. Serve hot.

Ideal for serving with Indian curries on special occasions.

SAFFRON RICE
Serves 4

- *1 tablespoon ghee*
- *4 cardamom pods, bruised*
- *3 whole cloves*
- *1 small stick cinnamon*
- *2½ cups long grain rice or basmati rice*
- *4 cups chicken or lamb stock*
- *1 teaspoon salt or to taste*
- *¼ teaspoon saffron strands*

Melt ghee in heavy saucepan and gently fry cardamom pods, cloves and cinnamon for 3 minutes. Add rice and continue to fry, stirring, for another 3 minutes. Add stock and salt to rice and bring mixture to boil over high heat. Reduce heat to low; cover and cook for 10 minutes.

While rice cooks, toast saffron strands in a dry pan over low heat for 1 to 2 minutes, stirring frequently and taking care they don't darken and burn. Turn onto a saucer to cool and when crisp, crush to powder with back of a spoon. Dissolve in 2 tablespoons boiling water. Uncover pan and sprinkle saffron water over rice after it has cooked for 10 minutes. Do not stir. Replace lid and cook for a further 10 minutes. Remove lid so steam can escape. Fluff gently with a fork and remove cinnamon stick and any visible whole spices before serving.

A lovely pilau with slight sweetness which children will love.

SPICED PARSI RICE
Serves 6

- 2½ cups long grain rice or basmati rice
- 2 tablespoons ghee or unsalted butter
- 5 cardamom pods, bruised
- 1 small cinnamon stick
- 3 whole cloves
- salt to taste
- rind of an orange, finely grated
- 3 tablespoons sultanas
- 2 tablespoons sliced almonds, toasted
- ¼ cup roasted cashews

Wash rice if necessary and leave to drain until thoroughly dried. Heat ghee in a heavy based saucepan; add cardamom, cinnamon and cloves and fry gently for 2 minutes. Stir in rice and fry, stirring constantly, for 2 to 3 minutes. Add 1 L hot water, salt and orange rind. Stir well and bring quickly to boil. Turn heat very low, cover tightly, and cook for 15 minutes without lifting lid. At the end of this time sprinkle sultanas over surface of rice, replace lid and cook for 5 minutes more. Turn out onto serving plate, remove whole spices and garnish with almonds and cashews.

An ideal, one-dish family meal from China. While the flavours are delicate, accompanying sauces provide heat for those who need it.

HAINAN CHICKEN RICE
Serves 6

- 1.5 kg (3 lb) roasting chicken
- 1 onion
- 1 star anise
- few sprigs celery leaves
- ½ teaspoon whole black peppercorns
- 2 teaspoons salt
- ¼ cup peanut oil
- 2 tablespoons oriental sesame oil
- 1 finely sliced onion
- 1 tablespoon finely shredded fresh ginger
- 1 tablespoon finely sliced garlic
- 2½ cups long grain rice
- 1 tablespoon chicken stock powder, optional

Remove excess fat from chicken, cut off tail and wing tips.

Choose a saucepan just large enough to hold the chicken and enough water to cover. Bring 10 cups water to boil with whole onion, star anise, celery leaves, peppercorns and salt. Carefully put chicken into pan, breast downwards, so it is covered with water. When water returns to boil turn heat low, cover pan and simmer for 20 minutes. Without uncovering pan remove from heat and allow chicken to finish cooking in stored heat for a further 40 minutes.

Heat both oils in a heavy saucepan and fry sliced onion, ginger and garlic over low heat until soft and golden. Remove and reserve 2 tablespoons oil. Add rice and fry 2 minutes, stirring. Add 4 cups of strained chicken stock and chicken stock powder. When it returns to boil reduce heat to lowest setting, cover pan tightly and cook for 15 minutes.

Chop chicken into bite-size pieces, arrange on serving plate and keep warm. Serve rice and chicken accompanied by dipping sauces, strain remaining stock and serve as soup.

DIPPING SAUCES: Traditionally, two sauces are served with Hainan Chicken Rice. One is dark soy sauce with sliced chillies, the other is finely grated ginger mixed with reserved oil.

SAVOURY RICE AND LENTILS
Serves 4 to 6

- *1 cup long grain rice or basmati rice*
- *1 cup red lentils or moong dhal*
- *2 tablespoons ghee or butter*
- *2 onions, finely sliced*
- *1 teaspoon turmeric*
- *1½ teaspoons salt or to taste*
- *1 teaspoon garam masala (see p. 73)*

Wash rice and set aside to drain. Wash lentils or dhal thoroughly and leave to drain. Melt ghee in large saucepan and fry onion over low heat until golden brown, stirring from time to time. Remove half the onion and set aside. Stir in turmeric and fry for a few seconds. Add rice and lentils to pan and fry while stirring constantly for 1 or 2 minutes. Add 3½ cups hot water, salt and garam masala. Bring to boil, then reduce heat to very low, cover and cook for 20 minutes. Do not uncover while cooking. To serve, fluff with fork and garnish with reserved onion.

Crisp, crunchy noodles with an explosion of contrasting flavours—sweet, salty, sour. Though chilli and pickled garlic usually garnish the dish, for family meals serve them in a separate bowl.

CRISPY RICE NOODLES
Serves 6

- 250 g (8 oz) rice vermicelli
- 3 cups peanut oil for deep-frying
- 2 tablespoons white wine vinegar
- 2 tablespoons sugar
- 2 tablespoons fish sauce
- 125 g (4 oz) finely minced chicken or pork
- 125 g (4 oz) shelled, deveined and chopped raw prawns
- 1 cake firm bean curd, finely diced
- 2 eggs, beaten
- ½ cup fresh coriander leaves

Put rice vermicelli in a large paper or plastic bag and divide into small handfuls. Heat oil in a wok and test heat with a few strands of vermicelli. It should immediately puff, swelling to many times its size. If not, oil is not hot enough and vermicelli will be tough instead of crisp and light.

Fry a handful at a time, scooping out with wire strainer as soon as they puff and turn pale gold. Drain well on paper towels. Cool completely. Pour off most of the oil (may be re-used) leaving 2 tablespoons in wok.

Dissolve sugar in vinegar and fish sauce. Reheat oil in wok, add chicken or pork and stir-fry until colour changes. Add prawns and cook for 1 minute longer. Toss in bean curd and stir-fry until heated through. Add vinegar mixture and when it boils add beaten eggs. Stir constantly until egg is set and firm.. This may all be done beforehand. At serving time reheat the pork mixture. Turn off heat and combine with crisp-fried noodles. Sprinkle with coriander and serve while at its crispy best. Offer pickled garlic and sliced chillies separately.

Note If using an iron wok, do not leave meat/egg mixture standing in it after cooking or it will develop a metallic taste. I use and recommend an enamel wok.

Great for picnics and popular with old and young.

EGG NOODLE SALAD
Serves 4 to 6

- *250 g egg noodles*
- *2 tablespoons peanut oil*
- *2 tablespoons oriental sesame oil*
- *4 tablespoons light soy sauce*
- *1 clove garlic*
- *2 teaspoons sugar*
- *1 cup diced cooked ham*
- *1 cup diced cooked chicken*
- *¼ cup chopped spring onion*
- *¼ cup chopped fresh coriander*

Cook noodles in plenty of lightly salted boiling water until just tender. Run cold water into pan and drain well. Combine oils, soy sauce, garlic crushed with sugar and pour over noodles in a bowl. Add remaining ingredients, toss to mix and serve at room temperature.

Rice noodles are popular in Thailand and the dried varieties come in a range of thicknesses. When flatter and thicker, they are known as rice sticks.

RICE NOODLES WITH CHICKEN
Serves 4

- *250 g (8 oz) rice sticks*
- *250 g (8 oz) chicken fillets*
- *1 tablespoon fish sauce*
- *1 tablespoon lime juice*
- *2 teaspoons sugar*
- *3 tablespoons peanut oil*
- *2 cloves garlic, finely chopped*
- *1 teaspoon Maggi Seasoning (see Note)*
- *½ cup diagonally sliced spring onions*
- *½ cup roasted, salted peanuts, chopped*

Cover rice sticks with boiling water and soak for 10 minutes. Drain. Cut chicken into thin strips. Combine fish sauce, lime juice and sugar, stirring until sugar dissolves.

Heat oil in a wok or heavy frying pan and fry garlic on low heat until golden. Add chicken and stir-fry until it changes colour. Stir in Maggi Seasoning. Pour in sauce mixture and add drained rice noodles, tossing until well mixed. Mix in half the spring onions and peanuts and serve hot, garnished with remainder.

Note Maggi Seasoning is very similar in flavour to a Thai ingredient, Golden Mountain Sauce, and a lot more readily obtainable in Western supermarkets.

*In India these wonderful-tasting loaves (tandoori naan) are baked
in a charcoal-fired clay oven known as a tandoor.*

PUNJABI BREAD
Makes 8

- 1 sachet dried yeast or 30 g (1 oz) fresh yeast
- 1 tablespoon sugar
- ⅓ cup yoghurt
- 1 egg, beaten
- ¼ cup melted ghee or butter
- 2 teaspoons salt
- about 4 cups plain white flour
- extra yoghurt (about ¼ cup)
- ½ teaspoon crushed garlic, optional
- 2 tablespoons poppy seeds or kalonji (nigella) seeds

Pour ¼ cup warm water into a warm bowl and sprinkle yeast
over. Leave for a few minutes to soften, then stir until dissolved.
Stir in 1 teaspoon of the sugar and leave in a warm place
for 10 minutes, or until it bubbles. Beat yoghurt until smooth
and mix in remaining sugar, egg, ghee, salt and ½ cup lukewarm
water. Add yeast mixture and stir.

Put half the flour in a large bowl, make a well in the
centre and pour in liquid mixture, beating with a wooden
spoon until smooth. Stir in remaining flour a little at a time
and when mixture is too stiff to stir, knead with hands until
a firm dough. Knead on lightly floured board for 10 to 12
minutes, or until dough is smooth and elastic. Make dough
into ball, transfer to a warmed, greased bowl, turning it so
top surface is greased. Cover and leave in warm spot for an
hour or until doubled in bulk and a finger pushed into dough
leaves its impression. Punch down and divide into 8 balls.
Leave to rest further 10 minutes.

Preheat 2 ungreased baking sheets in very hot oven—
230°C (450°F). Shape dough into rounds, making them thinner
in centre than around rims. Pull one end of each circle to
elongate, forming traditional teardrop shape. Spread with extra
yoghurt (mixed with crushed garlic if this flavour is desired)
and sprinkle lightly with seeds. Bake 2 or 3 loaves on each
preheated tray for 10 minutes or until puffed and golden brown.
Serve warm.

These discs of Indian unleavened bread have a chewy texture and delicious flavour. An ideal partner to roasted and skewered dishes, dry vegetable preparations and lentil dishes.

CHAPATIS
Makes 20

- 3 cups atta flour or roti flour (see Note)
- 1 teaspoon salt, or to taste
- 1 cup lukewarm water

Reserve ½ cup flour for rolling out chapatis. Combine salt and remaining flour. Add water all at once, mixing to a firm, but not stiff dough. Knead dough for 10 minutes. It can also be made in a food processor, shortening kneading time. Form into ball, wrap and allow to stand for 1 hour.

Divide into walnut-size balls. Using reserved flour, roll out each one on a lightly floured board to a thin circle the size of a bread and butter plate. (It is best not to stack rolled chapatis on top of each other. If you must, sprinkle generously with flour between layers.) When chapatis are rolled, heat griddle plate or heavy frying pan until very hot, reduce heat and cook chapatis, starting with those rolled first (resting time makes chapatis lighter). Place chapati on griddle and leave for about 1 minute before turning on other side for another minute. Pressing edges lightly with a folded tea towel encourages rising.

Note For lighter chapatis, I suggest equal quantities of atta flour and plain white (all purpose) flour. For softer chapatis, rub a tablespoon of ghee or butter into flour before adding water.

PURIS
Makes 30

Use chapati dough, but make puris a little smaller, about the circumference of a teacup. Heat 2.5 cm (1 inch) depth of oil and when a faint haze rises, fry one at a time over medium heat. To make them puff up, spoon oil over puri continually as it cooks. Fry other side in the same way. When golden on both sides, drain on absorbent paper. Good with curries but try them with Semolina Pudding (see p. 83) for a sweet treat.

A rich, flaky bread based on chapati dough.

PARATHAS
Makes 10 to 12

- *1 quantity chapati dough (see p. 19)*
- *6 to 8 tablespoons melted ghee or butter*

Divide dough into 10 to 12 equal portions and roll each into a ball. Roll out one at a time on a lightly floured surface to a very thin circle. Brush with melted ghee and roll up like a Swiss roll. Coil tightly, then roll out again to a circle not quite as large as the first. Repeat with remaining dough. Cook on lightly greased griddle, spooning a little melted ghee on each side, until golden brown. Serve warm with Chicken Himalaya (page 40) and other Indian dishes.

These smooth-skinned buns are a nice change from rice when served with Chinese dishes.

STEAMED CHINESE BUNS
Makes 12

- *1 x 7 g sachet dry yeast*
- *1 teaspoon sugar*
- *2 cups self-raising flour*
- *½ cup plain flour*
- *1 tablespoon lard*
- *2 tablespoons caster sugar*

Dissolve yeast and sugar in 1 cup warm water. Leave in a warm place until frothy. Put both flours and caster sugar in a large bowl and rub in lard until well distributed. Add yeast mixture and stir to form a dough, turn onto a floured surface and knead for 5 minutes, adding as little flour as necessary to keep dough from sticking. Return dough to a warm, greased bowl, cover and leave in a warm place until double in size. Punch down and allow to rise for a further 30 minutes.

Shape into neat balls, arrange on squares of oiled greaseproof paper and allow to rise for 15 minutes. Place 6 in steamer, not touching, and steam over boiling water for 12 to 15 minutes. If a two-tiered steamer is available steam all at once. Leave covered for 2 minutes after turning off heat. Serve warm.

FISH

The dislike children often show for fish has less to do with flavour and more to do with bones. When buying fish for family meals it is best to choose cutlets, steaks and fillets which have had bones removed, or at least varieties which do not have very fine bones.

It is up to the adult who prepares the meal to make darned sure there are no tiny sharp bones left in the fillet (yes, some fillets do have bones) and to this end, familiarise yourself with the skeletal structure of the particular fish you are handling. Run a searching finger down the centre of the fillet, be very careful because a child need only choke once and he or she can be put off fish for life—or for a very long time, anyway. I should know, I still have vivid memories of such an incident and still approach eating fish with a great deal of caution.

Mildly spicy.

FISH CURRY WITH TOMATO
Serves 4 to 6

- 750 g (1½ lb) fish fillets or steaks
- 2 tablespoons ghee or oil
- 2 medium onions, finely chopped
- 2 teaspoons crushed garlic
- 2 teaspoons fresh ginger, chopped or grated
- 2 teaspoons ground coriander
- 1 teaspoon ground cummin
- 1 teaspoon ground turmeric
- 1 cup chopped ripe tomato or canned tomato
- salt to taste
- 1 teaspoon sugar
- 1½ teaspoons garam masala (see p. 73)
- squeeze of lime or lemon juice
- 2 tablespoons roughly chopped fresh coriander or mint

Wash fish and dry with paper towels. Cut into serving pieces. Heat ghee or oil in saucepan and fry onion, garlic and ginger over low heat, stirring constantly, until onion is soft and golden. Add coriander, cummin and turmeric and stir for a few minutes until spices are cooked.

Add tomato, salt, sugar and garam masala and cook, stirring, until reduced to pulp. Add fish to pan, spooning sauce over. Cover and simmer for 10 minutes, or until fish turns opaque and flakes easily when pierced with knife. Remove from heat, add lime juice and chopped herbs and stir through. Serve with rice.

PIQUANT STEAMED FISH
Serves 4

- *500 g (1 lb) white fish fillets or cutlets of choice*
- *salt to taste*
- *1 teaspoon oriental sesame oil*
- *1 teaspoon finely grated fresh ginger*
- *6 spring onions, finely sliced on diagonal*

SAUCE
- *1 rounded teaspoon dried tamarind*
- *1 tablespoon peanut oil*
- *1 small clove garlic, finely chopped*
- *1 tablespoon finely shredded ginger*
- *2 teaspoons palm sugar or brown sugar*

Rub fish fillets with salt mixed with grated ginger and sesame oil. Let stand while making sauce.

Soak dried tamarind in $1/3$ cup hot water for 10 minutes, then rub to dissolve pulp in water and strain out fibres before starting to make sauce.

Heat oil in small pan and fry garlic for a few seconds, stirring constantly until soft but not brown. Add shredded ginger and spring onions; cook for a few seconds longer, or until they are soft. Stir in sugar, tamarind liquid and ¼ cup water. Bring to boil.

Arrange fish on lightly oiled heatproof dish, scatter spring onions over and steam until done—the flesh will become opaque and flake easily when pierced with a knife. Do not overcook. Transfer to serving dish, spoon sauce over, garnish with coriander leaves and serve with steamed long grain rice.

FRIED FISH
Serves 4

- *500 g (1 lb) firm white fish fillets*
- *¼ cup plain flour*
- *¼ cup chickpea flour (besan)*
- *salt to taste*
- *½ teaspoon ground turmeric*
- *1 teaspoon garam masala (see p. 73)*
- *oil for frying*
- *1 egg, beaten well*

Wash fillets and dry on paper towels. Mix together flours, salt, turmeric and garam masala. Dip fish into beaten egg, then toss in flour mixture. Heat oil in deep frying pan. Fry fish fillets quickly until golden brown. Drain on paper towels and serve with Savoury Fried Potatoes (see p. 62) or boiled rice and pickles of choice.

Accompany this aromatic Thai dish with hot white rice and garnish with fresh chilli slices if desired.

STEAMED FISH PUDDING
Serves 4 to 6

- *500 g (1 lb) white fish fillets*
- *2 teaspoons Mild Red Curry Paste (see p. 71)*
- *1½ cups canned coconut milk*
- *2 eggs, lightly beaten*
- *1 tablespoon fish sauce*
- *salt to taste*
- *½ cup tightly packed basil leaves*
- *1 tablespoon rice flour*
- *1 kaffir lime leaf, shredded very finely*
- *coriander leaves*

Clean fish carefully, removing skin and all bones. Chop into pieces and place in food processor with curry paste. Process until puréed. Transfer to a bowl and gradually add ¾ cup of coconut milk, stirring well into fish mixture. Mix in beaten eggs, fish sauce and salt until well combined.

Spread basil leaves over base of large heatproof dish and spoon fish mixture over them. Tap container gently to settle contents. Place dish on steaming rack, cover and steam over boiling water for 20 minutes or until firm. Combine remaining coconut milk with rice flour in small saucepan, stir and cook until thickened. Remove steamer from heat and pour coconut milk mixture over surface of fish pudding. Scatter shredded lime leaf on top and return steamer to heat. Cook pudding for further 5 minutes. Remove from heat and allow to cool slightly and firm before serving. Garnish with coriander leaves and, for those who wish, chilli slices.

With this Thai dish you can steam, grill or fry the fish—or cook it in the microwave—but the most important thing is not to overcook. For family members who like heat, add some finely sliced fresh red chilli to the garnish.

Fish with Coconut Sauce
Serves 4

- 4 fillets or cutlets of fish of your choice
- 2 tablespoons lime or lemon juice
- 1 tablespoon fish sauce
- ⅔ cup canned coconut milk
- 1 tablespoon rice flour
- salt to taste
- finely sliced purple onion
- chopped coriander leaves

Cook fish until just done and transfer to serving plates. Sprinkle with lime juice and fish sauce. Mix coconut milk with ⅓ cup water, rice flour and salt in small saucepan. Stir over low heat until mixture thickens. Spoon coconut sauce over fish and garnish with purple onion slices and coriander leaves.

This North Indian dish is aromatic without being too fiery. Serve it hot with rice and accompanied by pickles for those who crave extra heat.

FISH IN SPICED YOGHURT
Serves 4 to 6

- *750 g (1½ lb) fish fillets*
- *salt and freshly ground black pepper to taste*
- *1 teaspoon ground turmeric*
- *oil for frying*
- *2 medium onions, roughly chopped*
- *2 cloves garlic*
- *3 teaspoons chopped fresh ginger*
- *2 tablespoons ground almonds*
- *3 teaspoons ground coriander*
- *2 teaspoons ground cummin*
- *1 teaspoon garam masala (see p. 73)*
- *½ cup plain yoghurt*
- *1 tablespoon chopped fresh mint leaves*

Wash fillets, dry and cut into large chunks, removing any bones. Combine salt, pepper and turmeric and rub over fish. Heat oil for shallow frying. Seal fish quickly on both sides over high heat. Transfer to plate.

Purée onions, garlic, ginger, almonds and spices in blender, adding a little water if necessary to keep mixture moving. Drain all but 2 tablespoons oil from pan and fry purée, stirring constantly, until colour changes and it smells fragrant.

Swirl ¼ cup water in blender to catch any traces of spices, stir into yoghurt and add. Simmer for a few minutes. Return fish pieces, turning gently to coat with sauce. Add salt to taste. Simmer, covered, for 10 minutes. Serve hot sprinkled with chopped mint and accompanied by rice.

Serve this creamy prawn curry with plain or spiced rice.

PRAWN CURRY WITH CREAM
Serves 4 to 6

- 750 g (1½ lb) raw prawns
- 3 onions
- 1 clove garlic, chopped
- 2 teaspoons chopped fresh ginger
- 1 teaspoon ground turmeric
- 3 tablespoons oil
- 1 large ripe tomato, peeled and chopped
- 1 teaspoon palm sugar or raw sugar
- 1 teaspoon salt
- ½ cup canned coconut milk
- ½ cup cream
- 1 teaspoon garam masala (see p. 73)
- 2 tablespoons chopped fresh coriander leaves

Shell and devein prawns. Roughly chop onions and purée in blender with garlic, ginger and turmeric.

Heat oil in a heavy saucepan and fry purée until fragrant, stirring for about 5 minutes. Stir in tomato, palm sugar, salt, coconut milk, cream and ¼ cup water. Stir until boiling and simmer for 5 minutes. Add prawns and simmer until prawns turn pink and opaque—about 5 minutes. Do not overcook. Stir in garam masala and coriander leaves and serve immediately.

Make these lightly seasoned seafood patties with fish in season or prawns, depending on availability and budget. Or mix both together.

FISH OR PRAWN CAKES
Serves 4

- *500 g (1 lb) firm white fish fillets*
or shelled raw prawns or some of each
- *½ cup finely chopped celery or water chestnuts*
- *4 spring onions, finely shredded*
- *1 teaspoon grated fresh ginger*
- *salt to taste*
- *white pepper to taste*
- *2 tablespoons cornflour*
- *2 tablespoons coriander leaves, chopped*
- *3 eggs, lightly beaten*
- *peanut oil for frying*

DIPPING SAUCE
- *1 teaspoon sugar*
- *2 tablespoons light soy sauce*
- *1 tablespoon rice vinegar or white wine vinegar*
- *1 teaspoon grated ginger*

Carefully remove skin and any bones from fish fillets, or devein prawns. Finely mince or chop fish or prawn meat. Combine with remaining ingredients, except oil. Mix thoroughly.

Heat a heavy frying pan and add just enough oil to film base. Fry large spoonfuls of mixture until golden, then turn to cook other side. Remove from pan and keep warm. Repeat with remaining mixture, oiling pan as necessary, until all mixture is cooked. Serve warm with Dipping Sauce.

DIPPING SAUCE Stir all ingredients together in a small bowl until sugar is dissolved.

Include your family's favourite vegetables in this recipe. Some you might consider are Chinese cabbage, broccoli, spring onions, beans, baby corn, snow peas or sugar snap peas, mushrooms and carrots.

STIR-FRIED PRAWNS WITH VEGETABLES AND OYSTER SAUCE

Serves 4

- 500 g (1 lb) raw prawns
- 3 tablespoons peanut oil
- 1 teaspoon crushed garlic
- ½ teaspoon finely grated fresh ginger
- 3 cups vegetables, cut into bite-size pieces
- 2 tablespoons oyster sauce
- 2 tablespoons dry sherry
- 2 teaspoons cornflour

Shell and devein prawns. Heat 1 tablespoon oil in wok and stir-fry vegetables until tender but still crunchy. Transfer to dish.

Add remaining oil to wok and fry garlic and ginger over low heat, stirring constantly, until soft and golden. Add prawns and stir-fry over medium heat until they turn pink and curl. Add oyster sauce, sherry, ½ cup water and bring to boil. Mix cornflour with 1 tablespoon cold water. Add to liquid in wok and cook, stirring, until sauce thickens and clears. Return vegetables to mix with prawns and sauce until heated through. Do not overcook prawns and vegetables. Serve immediately with hot white rice.

EGG DISHES

If you'd like to add a little fire to this Indian dish, first cook half the mixture as directed . . . for the children. Then add seeded and chopped fresh red or green chillies, cooking them with the spring onions (and that's Dad's and Mum's). Since scrambled eggs are so quick to cook, it's no big deal to make two versions.

SPICY SCRAMBLED EGGS
Serves 4 to 6

- 6 to 8 eggs
- ¼ cup milk
- salt and ground black pepper to taste
- ½ teaspoon ground cummin
- 2 tablespoons chopped fresh mint or coriander leaves
- 2 tablespoons ghee
- 6 spring onions, finely chopped
- 1 teaspoon fresh grated ginger
- ⅛ teaspoon ground turmeric
- 1 large ripe tomato, diced

Beat eggs until mixed together. Stir in milk, salt, pepper, cummin and coriander or mint. Heat ghee in a large, heavy frying pan and cook spring onions and ginger slowly until soft. Add turmeric and tomato and fry, stirring, for 1 to 2 minutes more. Add egg mixture and cook over low heat, stirring and lifting eggs as they begin to set. Cook until eggs are creamy—be careful not to let them get dry. Serve with Indian bread.

A favourite South Indian dish, popular throughout South-East Asia as a luncheon for children, served with steamed rice. If desired you can add a whole fresh green chilli, simmering it with the coconut milk. It will impart flavour without heat. (Just remember to fish it out before serving!)

Eggs in Coconut Milk Sauce
Serves 4 to 6

- 6 eggs
- 2 tablespoons oil
- 2 medium onions, finely sliced
- 3 cloves garlic, chopped finely
- 2 teaspoons finely grated fresh ginger
- 6 curry leaves
- 1 teaspoon ground turmeric
- 1½ cups canned coconut milk
- salt to taste
- 2 tablespoons lime or lemon juice

Hard-boil eggs, then cool in bowl of iced water. Shell and set aside. Heat oil over low heat and fry onion, garlic, ginger and curry leaves, stirring frequently, until onions are soft. Do not let them brown. Add turmeric and stir for a few seconds, then stir in ½ cup of coconut milk mixed with 1½ cups water. Simmer gently, uncovered, for 10 minutes.

Add remaining coconut milk and salt to pan and stir

constantly until it returns to simmering point. Halve eggs and add to pan, spooning some of the sauce over. Simmer, uncovered, for a further 5 minutes. Remove from heat and stir in lime or lemon juice. Serve immediately.

Chilli lovers can garnish this Thai dish with sliced fresh chillies (as an optional extra), but even without them the dish is unusually tasty.

EGGS IN TAMARIND SAUCE
Serves 4 to 6

- 6 eggs
- ¼ cup peanut oil
- 2 medium onions, thinly sliced
- 2 tablespoons palm sugar or brown sugar
- 1 teaspoon instant tamarind pulp
- 1 tablespoon fish sauce
- coriander leaves

Place eggs in saucepan of cold water and bring to boil, stirring gently to centre yolks. Simmer for 10 minutes, then place eggs in cold water until quite cold. Shell eggs and wipe dry with paper towel. Make some punctures with a very fine toothpick to prevent them bursting when fried.

Heat oil and fry eggs in a wok until crisp and golden. Drain on paper towel. Pour off all but 1 tablespoon of oil, reheat and stir-fry onions until golden and slightly crisp. Remove from wok and drain on paper. Mix palm sugar, tamarind pulp and fish sauce with 3 tablespoons water. Stir over low heat for 5 minutes or until syrupy. Pour over eggs and serve sprinkled with fried onions and coriander leaves. Accompany with rice.

STIR-FRIED EGGS WITH VEGETABLES
Serves 4 to 6

- 4 eggs
- salt to taste
- 250 g (8 oz) Chinese cabbage (wongah bak)
- 60 g (2 oz) button mushrooms
- 1 carrot
- 4 spring onions
- 2 tablespoons peanut oil
- ½ teaspoon finely grated fresh ginger
- 1 small clove garlic, finely chopped
- 1 tablespoon light soy sauce
- ½ teaspoon sugar
- 1 teaspoon oriental sesame oil

Beat eggs and salt together. Halve cabbage leaves lengthways, stack and shred finely. Wipe mushrooms, trim stems and slice. Cut carrot into matchstick strips. Cut spring onions diagonally.

Heat 1 tablespoon peanut oil in a wok. Pour in eggs and stir-fry until set. Transfer to plate. Wipe out wok and heat remaining peanut oil. Add ginger and garlic and stir-fry for a few seconds. Add cabbage, mushrooms and carrot and stir-fry for 1 minute. Cover wok and cook for 1 to 2 minutes until vegetables are half cooked. Add spring onions, soy sauce, sugar and sesame oil. Cover and cook over low heat for 1 minute. Toss through cooked eggs and serve immediately.

STEAMED EGG WITH MUSHROOMS
Serves 4

- 4 dried shiitake (Chinese) mushrooms
- 60 g (2 oz) bean thread vermicelli
- 125 g (4 oz) fresh, frozen or canned crabmeat
- 125 g (4 oz) barbecued or roast pork
- 5 eggs
- 2 spring onions, finely chopped
- 2 teaspoons fresh coriander leaves, finely chopped
- salt and black pepper to taste

Soak mushrooms in hot water for 30 minutes. Take a small amount of bean thread vermicelli and soak in hot water for 10 minutes, then drain and measure out ½ cup. Drain and flake crabmeat, discarding any bony tissue. Chop pork finely. Squeeze excess water from mushrooms, discard stems and slice caps thinly.

Beat eggs with fork until blended but not frothy. Stir in chopped spring onions, coriander, salt, pepper, mushrooms, noodles, crabmeat and pork. Pour into heatproof dish and steam, covered, on a trivet in large pan of boiling water until firm—cooking time will depend on depth of mixture in dish. Serve with rice.

GARLIC, CHILLI AND FISH SAUCE

- 2 ripe red chillies
- 1 clove garlic, finely chopped
- 1 tablespoon sugar
- 1 lime
- 1 tablespoon vinegar
- 4 tablespoons fish sauce

Cut off stalks from chillies, split down centre and remove seeds with point of a sharp knife. Chop finely or pound in a mortar and pestle with garlic. Add sugar. Cut lime in half and squeeze on a citrus juicer. Discard seeds but add juice and pulp to chillies. Stir in vinegar, fish sauce and 2 tablespoons water. Serve with eggs for those who want a touch of heat.

Most often served cold as part of a hors-d'oeuvre selection, this tasty and nutritious combination of chicken and eggs is an ideal introduction to oriental flavours for youngsters. Serve with rice and lightly cooked green vegetables for a complete meal.

STEAMED EGG ROLL
Serves 4

FILLING
- 185 g (6 oz) raw lean chicken, roughly chopped
- salt to taste
- 2 teaspoons light soy sauce
- ½ teaspoon oriental sesame oil
- ½ teaspoon finely grated fresh ginger
- ½ teaspoon crushed garlic
- 1 teaspoon cornflour
- 2 tablespoons finely chopped spring onions

WRAPPERS
- 4 eggs
- salt to taste
- 1 tablespoon peanut oil
- 1 teaspoon oriental sesame oil

In food processor combine chopped chicken with salt, soy sauce, sesame oil, ginger and garlic and process in short bursts until smooth, stopping and mixing mixture with spatula as necessary. Add cornflour and spring onions, and process again. (Alternatively, chop all ingredients together with sharp chopper until mixture forms paste.)

WRAPPERS Beat eggs with salt. Reserve 1 tablespoon to seal egg rolls. Heat small omelette pan; oil with paper towel dipped in both oils mixed together. Use 2 to 3 tablespoons of egg to make a thin omelette, cooking on one side. Flip onto a board. Repeat with remaining mixture to make 4 or 5 omelettes.

Divide filling according to number of omelettes. Spread filling almost to edges of the cooked side of each omelette with oiled spatula. Roll up Swiss Roll style, seal with reserved beaten egg. Lightly grease a plate and arrange rolls on it in single layer. Cover and steam over boiling water for 15 minutes. Allow to cool a little before cutting into diagonal slices. Serve hot or cold.

OMELETTE CURRY
Serves 4

- *6 eggs*
- *salt and pepper to taste*
- *2 tablespoons butter*
- *3 tablespoons finely chopped onion*
- *2 teaspoons chopped fresh dill*
- *1 quantity Coconut Milk Sauce (see p. 33)*

Beat eggs slightly, season with salt and pepper. Heat butter in a large non-stick frying pan and cook onion until soft and golden. Stir in dill and pour in beaten eggs. As eggs set, pull to centre of pan and let uncooked egg run out to edges. Fold omelette over from both sides to centre. It will be nice and thick. Cut in slices and simer gently in Coconut Milk Sauce for a few minutes. Serve with rice.

POULTRY AND MEATS

Familiar main dishes such as roast chicken and roast lamb can be given exotic flavours which prepare the way for more adventurous eating by even the youngest family members.

In traditional Chinese cooking the whole cooked chicken is placed on a chopping board and cut in halves lengthwise with a sharp cleaver. Each half is then cut across into 3.5 cm (1½ inch) strips. However, you can simply carve the chicken into joints to serve.

SPICED ROAST CHICKEN
Serves 6

- 1.75 kg (3½ lb) roasting chicken
- ¹/₃ cup dark soy sauce
- 2 tablespoons peanut oil
- 1 tablespoon dry sherry
- 1 teaspoon crushed garlic
- 1 teaspoon finely grated fresh ginger
- 1 teaspoon five spice powder
- 2 tablespoons honey

Wash chicken, removing excess fat and dry with paper towel. Combine remaining ingredients in baking dish. Coat chicken with marinade, spooning some into interior. Marinate for 1 hour. Roast in oven preheated to 180°C (350°F) for 1¾ hours, or until juice runs clear, not pink, when skewer is inserted in thigh. Turn and baste chicken when cooking. Finish cooking breast up. Serve hot or cold.

Serve this whole roast chicken warm or cold and accompanied by rice, Indian bread and/or salad.

CHICKEN HIMALAYA
Serves 6

- *1.5 kg (3 lb) roasting chicken*
- *1 teaspoon crushed garlic*
- *1 teaspoon finely grated fresh ginger*
- *1 tablespoon mild curry powder*
- *1 teaspoon paprika*
- *salt to taste*
- *1 teaspoon garam masala (see p. 73)*
- *2 tablespoons lime or lemon juice*
- *1 tablespoon soy sauce*
- *2 tablespoons peanut or oriental sesame oil*
- *2 tablespoons ground rice*

Wash chicken, removing excess fat, and dry well. Combine remaining ingredients to make a paste of spreading consistency. Rub over chicken inside and out and marinate 1 hour.

Roast in oven preheated to 180°C (350°F) for 1¼ hours or until chicken is done. If surface browns too quickly during roasting, cover loosely with foil. Serve with rice or flat bread, and salad.

CHICKEN AND PINEAPPLE
Serves 4

- *425 g (15 oz) can unsweetened pineapple pieces*
- *375 g (12 oz) chicken breast fillets*
- *1 tablespoon cornflour*
- *salt to taste*
- *black pepper to taste*
- *1 tablespoon light soy sauce*
- *2 teaspoons oriental sesame oil*
- *½ teaspoon crushed garlic*
- *1 teaspoon finely grated fresh ginger*
- *1 tablespoon peanut oil*
- *4 spring onions, sliced on diagonal*

SAUCE
- *2 teaspoons cornflour*
- *½ cup pineapple juice*
- *1 tablespoon light soy sauce*

Drain pineapple, reserving juice for sauce. Cut chicken into thin slices, then toss in cornflour mixed with salt and pepper until well coated. Add soy sauce, sesame oil, garlic and ginger and mix with chicken.

In wok, heat peanut oil. Add chicken and stir-fry just until colour changes. Add pineapple, lower heat, cover and simmer for 3 minutes. Gradually add pineapple juice to cornflour, mixing until smooth. Stir in soy sauce.

Add this sauce mixture to wok, stirring until it thickens. Toss in spring onions and mix through. Serve immediately with rice or noodles.

'Red cooking' refers to cooking in dark soy sauce. Chicken drumsticks cooked in this manner make ideal picnic food. Freeze or refrigerate leftover cooking liquid. If refrigerating, keep this 'Master Sauce' alive by cooking meat or poultry in it at least once a week.

RED-COOKED CHICKEN DRUMSTICKS
Serves 4 to 6

- *2 kg (4 lb) chicken drumsticks*
- *1½ cups dark soy sauce*
- *½ cup dry sherry*
- *5 cm (2 inch) piece fresh ginger, sliced*
- *1 clove garlic, bruised*
- *10 small sections star anise*
- *1 tablespoon sugar*
- *2 teaspoons oriental sesame oil*

Wash drumsticks and dry on paper towels. Place in saucepan or flameproof casserole just large enough so that chicken is covered with the cooking sauce. Add 1½ cups water and remaining ingredients, except sesame oil. Bring slowly to boil, cover pan and simmer gently for 30 minutes or until tender.

With tongs, turn drumsticks over during cooking. If any pieces are not submerged, rearrange during cooking time. Turn off heat and leave to cool in covered saucepan. Lift chicken pieces from sauce and transfer to serving platter. Brush with sesame oil and serve at room temperature with a small amount of cooking liquid for dipping.

CHICKEN WITH ALMONDS AND BROCCOLI
Serves 6

- 750 g (1½ lb) chicken breast fillets
  - 3 teaspoons cornflour
  - 1 teaspoon five spice powder
    - salt to taste
    - peanut oil
  - 1 cup blanched almonds
  - 1 tablespoon dry sherry
  - 1 tablespoon light soy sauce
    - 1 teaspoon sugar
    - 2 teaspoons cornflour
  - 125 g (4 oz) broccoli florets
- 1 teaspoon finely grated fresh ginger
  - ½ teaspoon crushed garlic

Cut chicken into 1 cm (½ inch) squares. Mix cornflour, five spice powder and salt together. Sprinkle over chicken and mix well. Deep-fry almonds over medium heat until golden, stirring constantly. Drain on paper towels. Pour off oil and wipe out wok with paper towel.

Stir together sherry, soy sauce, sugar, cornflour and 3 tablespoons cold water, until sugar dissolves. Heat 2 tablespoons peanut oil in wok and stir-fry broccoli over high heat for 2 minutes. Transfer to plate. Add another 2 tablespoons oil and fry ginger and garlic for a few seconds. Toss in chicken and

43

fry, stirring, until chicken changes colour—1 to 2 minutes. Stir reserved sauce mixture and add to wok, stirring until liquid boils and thickens. Mix in almonds and broccoli and serve immediately with rice.

A popular dish with children. Add a few chunks of a favourite vegetable when steaming the chicken and serve hot with rice.

SIMPLE STEAMED CHICKEN
Serves 4 to 5

- *1 kg (2 lb) chicken pieces*
- *3 teaspoons light soy sauce*
- *2 teaspoons dry sherry*
- *2 teaspoons cornflour*
- *1 teaspoon finely grated fresh ginger*
- *½ teaspoon salt*
- *1 teaspoon sugar*
- *1 teaspoon oriental sesame oil*

Using sharp, heavy cleaver, cut chicken into bite-size pieces, chopping straight through meat and bones. Wipe cuts with damp paper towel to remove any small splinters of bone. Mix chicken with remaining ingredients.

Place on shallow dish (such as a pie plate) in steamer. If you don't own a steamer, improvise one with an upturned bowl or trivet in a large pan of boiling water. (Add slow cooking vegetables at this point and those which cook quicker later on.) Cover and steam over boiling water for 15 minutes. Serve with rice.

The flavours in this dish were made for children—even toddlers love to pick up the wings and nibble.

HONEY SOY CHICKEN WINGS
Serves 6 to 8

- 1.5 kg (3 lb) chicken wings
- ⅓ cup dark soy sauce
- 2 tablespoons honey
- 2 tablespoons dry sherry
- 2 tablespoons peanut oil
- 2 teaspoons oriental sesame oil
- 1 clove garlic, crushed
- 1 teaspoon finely grated fresh ginger
- ½ teaspoon five spice powder
- fresh coriander leaves

Wash and dry wings, cut off and discard wing tips. Combine all other ingredients and marinate the wings for 1 hour. Place in a single layer in roasting dish. Roast in preheated moderate oven, 180°C (350°F), for 35 minutes. Turn wings over using tongs, brush with any remaining marinade and roast for further 20 minutes or until wings are brown and glazed. Serve warm, garnished with coriander leaves and accompanied by rice.

Substitute oranges or tangelo for mandarins when the latter are out of season. The Szechwan peppercorns used in this dish aren't hot in the same way as black peppercorns or chilli. Serve chilli sauce separately for those who like extra heat. This dish can be cooked ahead and reheated just before serving.

Braised Mandarin Chicken
Serves 6

- 1.5 kg (3 lb) roasting chicken
- 1 mandarin or substitute
- 1 teaspoon Szechwan peppercorns
- 2 tablespoons peanut oil
- 2 teaspoons finely chopped fresh ginger
- 3 spring onions, finely sliced
- salt to taste
- 2 teaspoons oriental sesame oil

Sauce
- ¼ cup mandarin or orange juice
- ¼ cup dry sherry
- 2 tablespoons dark soy sauce
- 2 teaspoons sugar
- 1 teaspoon oriental sesame oil

Cut chicken in half lengthwise and place on a wooden board cut side down. With a heavy, sharp cleaver chop each half into strips 2.5 cm (1 inch) wide. Wipe cuts with damp paper to remove any bits of bone.

Peel mandarin, remove all white pith from rind and cut rind into fine shreds. Toast peppercorns in dry pan until fragrant, then crush finely.

Heat peanut oil in wok. Add ginger and shredded rind, toss for a few seconds, then add half the chicken pieces, stir-frying over high heat until browned. Remove. Brown remaining chicken pieces. Return first half of chicken to wok, sprinkle with salt and Szechwan pepper. Combine sauce ingredients except sesame oil and pour into wok, stirring to mix. Cover wok and simmer for 30 minutes. Turn chicken pieces every 10 minutes so they cook evenly. Add spring onions. Cook over high heat, stirring, until sauce reduces and thickens. Remove from heat, mix in sesame oil and serve with hot steamed rice.

CITRUS CHICKEN AND PINE NUTS
Serves 4 to 6

- *750 g (1½ lb) chicken thigh fillets*
  - *1 teaspoon salt*
  - *1 tablespoon sherry*
    - *1 egg white*
  - *1 tablespoon cornflour*
  - *3 tablespoons peanut oil*
  - *30 g (1 oz) pine nuts*
- *1 teaspoon oriental sesame oil*
- *6 slices lemon or orange slices*

SAUCE
- *½ cup strained orange juice*
- *2 tablespoons lemon juice*
  - *1 tablespoon sugar*
- *2 teaspoons light soy sauce*
  - *1 tablespoon cornflour*

Remove any pockets of fat from chicken and cut meat into bite-size pieces. Season with salt and sherry, pour unbeaten egg white over and mix well. Leave for 10 minutes. Sprinkle with cornflour, add 1 tablespoon peanut oil and mix again. Cover and chill for at least 30 minutes.

Bring plenty of lightly salted water to boil in wok and drop in ⅓ of chicken pieces at a time, stirring until they turn white. Remove with slotted spoon and drain in colander. Repeat with remaining chicken.

Combine sauce ingredients with ½ cup water. Heat remaining oil in wok and fry pine nuts over medium heat until golden. Transfer to paper towel and wipe out wok. Stir reserved sauce mixture and pour into wok. Cook, stirring constantly, until it boils and thickens. Add sesame oil. Return chicken and pine nuts to wok, heat through and serve immediately garnished with orange or lemon slices.

BARBECUED OR GRILLED CHICKEN
Serves 4 to 6

- 1 kg (2 lb) chicken pieces
- 1 teaspoon grated ginger
- ½ teaspoon crushed garlic
- 1 teaspoon sugar
- ¼ teaspoon five spice powder
- 2 teaspoons oyster sauce
- 1 tablespoon hoi sin sauce
- 2 tablespoons soy sauce
- 2 tablespoons oil

Lightly score chicken pieces. Combine remaining ingredients and pour over chicken, mix well and marinate overnight. Grill, turning chicken during cooking and basting with any marinade remaining in bowl. Do not overcook! Cooking should take 15 to 20 minutes.

CHICKEN IN PEANUT SAUCE
Serves 6

- *1 kg (2 lb) chicken half-breasts on the bone*
  - *2 small cloves garlic, crushed*
  - *1 teaspoon finely grated fresh ginger*
- *1 tablespoon Mild Green Curry Paste (see p. 72)*
  - *2 tablespoons peanut oil*
  - *1 cup spring onions, cut into small pieces*
  - *3 tablespoons crunchy peanut butter*
  - *2 teaspoons palm sugar or brown sugar*
    - *1 tablespoon fish sauce*
    - *¾ cup canned coconut milk*
- *2 cups snake beans or green beans, cut into short lengths*

Chop each half-breast in two. Mix garlic, ginger and curry paste and rub into chicken pieces. Allow to marinate for 20 minutes.

Heat oil in wok. Add spring onions stirring for a few seconds, then remove. Fry chicken pieces, turning until evenly browned. Mix peanut butter, sugar, fish sauce and canned coconut milk with ½ cup water. (If your brand of coconut milk is very thin, don't add water but use more coconut milk.) Stir until sugar dissolves, pour into wok and bring to boil. Cover and cook gently until chicken is tender, stirring occasionally and adding a little water if sauce reduces too much. Blanch green beans, drain and add with spring onions to chicken. Gently mix together. Serve with steamed rice and a salad.

Serve this rich Indian curry with rice or flat bread.

CURRIED CHICKEN WITH CASHEWS
Serves 6

- *1.5 kg (3 lb) chicken pieces*
- *2 tablespoons ghee or oil*
- *3 medium onions, finely chopped*
- *2 cloves garlic, finely chopped*
- *1 teaspoon finely grated fresh ginger*
- *2 tablespoons mild curry powder*
- *1 teaspoon paprika*
- *salt to taste*
- *2 large ripe tomatoes, chopped*
- *2 tablespoons chopped fresh mint leaves*
- *1 teaspoon garam masala (see p. 73)*
- *½ cup plain yoghurt*
- *½ cup finely chopped raw cashews*

The smaller the chicken pieces, the more flavour they absorb. Use heavy cleaver when chopping pieces into smaller sizes as this makes it easier to cut through bones.

In large saucepan heat ghee or oil and cook onions, garlic and ginger over low heat, stirring occasionally, until onion is soft and golden. The slower the cooking, the better the flavour. Stir in curry powder and paprika, then add salt, tomatoes and mint. Cook until soft and pulpy, stirring frequently. Add chicken pieces and stir until well coated. Cover and simmer gently for 40 minutes or until chicken is tender. Stir often to prevent spices sticking to base of pan. Stir in garam masala and yoghurt and simmer, uncovered, for the last 5 minutes. Add cashews, mixing until heated. Serve sprinkled with extra mint if desired.

THAI CHICKEN WITH SNOW PEAS
Serves 4

- *500 g (1 lb) chicken thigh fillets*
- *125 g (4 oz) snow peas*
- *½ cup canned coconut milk*
- *2 tablespoons Mild Green Curry Paste (see p. 72)*
- *1 tablespoon fish sauce*
- *1 teaspoon palm sugar or brown sugar*
- *4 kaffir lime leaves*
- *¼ cup sweet basil leaves*

Trim excess fat from chicken and cut into bite-size pieces. Top and string snow peas.

Heat half the coconut milk in wok. When boiling add Mild Green Curry Paste and cook, stirring for a few minutes. Add fish sauce and chicken pieces and cook, stirring constantly, until chicken is well coated and no longer pink.

Mix remaining coconut milk with ½ cup water and add to wok with sugar and kaffir lime leaves. Simmer over low heat for 10 minutes. Add snow peas and basil and simmer a few minutes more. Serve with hot white rice.

A mild North Indian dish with a yoghurt-based gravy. Saffron imparts delicate fragrance. Worth making a large quantity as it freezes well.

LAMB KORMA
Serves 6 to 8

- 2 kg (4 lb) boned leg of lamb
- 4 medium onions, peeled
- 1 tablespoon chopped fresh ginger
- 1 tablespoon chopped garlic
- ¼ cup blanched almonds
- 1 tablespoon ground cummin
- 1 teaspoon ground turmeric
- 2 teaspoons garam masala (see p. 73)
- ½ teaspoon saffron strands
- 1 tablespoon ghee
- 2 tablespoons oil
- 2 teaspoons salt or to taste
- 1 cup plain yoghurt
- ¼ cup chopped fresh coriander leaves

Trim away excess fat and cut lamb into 5 cm (2 inch) cubes. Slice 2 onions thinly. Chop remaining onions and blend with ginger, garlic, almonds, ground cummin, turmeric and garam masala in food processor or blender. Add a little water if necessary until all ingredients form a smooth paste. Toast saffron in dry pan over gentle heat for 1 or 2 minutes, taking care the delicate strands do not scorch. Turn onto saucer and when cool and crisp, crush with back of a spoon and dissolve the powder in 2 tablespoons boiling water.

In large heavy saucepan or flameproof casserole heat ghee and oil and fry sliced onion, stirring frequently, until golden. Stir in blended mixture and continue to cook, stirring constantly, until oil begins to separate from mixture. Rinse food processor or blender container with ¼ cup water and add to pan with salt. Continue to cook, stirring, until liquid evaporates again. Add meat and stir over medium heat, coating each piece with spice mixture. Add yoghurt and saffron and stir. Lower heat, cover and simmer gently for 1 hour or until meat is tender and gravy thickened, stirring occasionally to prevent sticking to base of pan. Sprinkle with chopped coriander leaves, cover and cook for 5 minutes more. Serve hot with rice.

*This recipe will win fans with its gentle spicing and honeyed sweetness.
Leftovers will star in salads or sandwiches.*

KASHMIRI ROAST LAMB
Serves 8

- 2–2.5 kg (4–5 lb) leg of lamb
- 2 teaspoons finely grated fresh ginger
- 2 cloves garlic, crushed
- salt to taste
- 1 teaspoon ground cumin
- 1 teaspoon ground turmeric
- 1½ teaspoons garam masala (see p. 73)
- ½ teaspoon saffron strands
- 1 cup natural yoghurt
- 2 tablespoons ground almonds
- 1 tablespoon honey
- 2 tablespoons blanched pistachios, optional

Remove skin and excess fat from lamb. With tip of knife make
deep slits in lamb. Mix together ginger, garlic, salt and spices,
adding a little oil to facilitate spreading if mixture appears
too dry. Rub over lamb and into each slit.

Toast saffron strands in dry pan over low heat for 1 or
2 minutes, turn onto saucer and when cool and crisp, crush
with back of a spoon. Dissolve in 2 tablespoons boiling water.
Combine with yoghurt, almonds and honey. Place lamb in

large baking dish and spoon yoghurt purée over. Cover and place in refrigerator. Marinate lamb for 2 days if possible, or at least overnight.

Preheat oven to very hot, 230°C (450°F), and roast lamb in covered baking dish for 30 minutes. Lower heat to moderate, 180°C (350°F), and cook for further 2 hours or until lamb is cooked through. Uncover and leave lamb to cool to room temperature. Slice and serve with pocket bread and salad, or with steamed long grain rice.

A great recipe for barbecues, and if you want to prepare ahead. Cover tightly with plastic wrap and refrigerate for 3 or 4 days.

LAMB KEBABS
Serves 6 to 8

- *1.5 kg (3 lb) lean boneless lamb*
- *1 teaspoon crushed garlic*
- *1 teaspoon finely grated fresh ginger*
- *1 teaspoon salt or to taste*
- *ground black pepper to taste*
- *1 teaspoon ground turmeric*
- *2 teaspoons ground coriander*
- *1 teaspoon ground cummin*
- *1 tablespoon oriental sesame oil*
- *2 tablespoons peanut oil*
- *2 tablespoons lemon juice*

Cut meat into cubes, discarding fat. Mix remaining ingredients and add to lamb, stirring until each cube is coated. Cover with cling wrap and refrigerate for at least 3 hours, or as long as 3 days. Soak bamboo skewers in cold water at least 1 hour before use to prevent burning.

Thread meat on skewers, about 5 pieces on each and cook over barbecue or under preheated grill until meat is browned and crisp on all sides. Serve at once with flat bread or steamed rice and sliced onions and tomatoes.

STIR-FRIED LAMB WITH VEGETABLES
Serves 4

- 6 dried shiitake (Chinese) mushrooms
- 500 g (1 lb) lamb leg steaks or lamb fillets
- ½ teaspoon crushed garlic
- salt to taste
- 2 teaspoons grated fresh ginger
- 1 teaspoon oriental sesame oil
- 1 tablespoon dry sherry
- 1 egg white, slightly beaten
- cornflour
- 2 tablespoons peanut oil
- 2 sticks celery, sliced
- 1 cup snow peas or sugar snap peas, strings removed
- 1 white onion cut in wedges
- 2 tablespoons soy sauce
- 1 teaspoon sugar

Soak mushrooms in hot water for 30 minutes. Discard stalks and slice caps. Trim any fat from lamb, slice meat thinly and place in bowl. Combine garlic, salt, ginger, sesame oil, sherry, egg white and 1 tablespoon cornflour. Mix with lamb, cover and leave to marinate for 30 minutes.

Heat 1 tablespoon peanut oil and fry celery and mushroom slices for 1 minute, add snow peas and onion, fry a minute longer. Remove to plate. Add remaining oil to wok and when hot add lamb, tossing and stirring constantly. Mix together soy sauce, sugar and 1 teaspoon cornflour with ¼ cup water. Push meat aside, add sauce mixture and cook, stirring, until thickened. Return vegetables to wok and mix with lamb and sauce. Serve hot with rice or noodles.

A simplified version of the recipe which has proved popular in Chinese restaurants.

MONGOLIAN LAMB
Serves 4

- *375 g (12 oz) lamb fillet*
- *2 tablespoons beaten egg*
- *½ teaspoon salt*
- *2 teaspoons sugar*
- *1 teaspoon crushed garlic*
- *1 tablespoon dark soy sauce*
- *1 teaspoon cornflour*
- *3 tablespoons peanut oil*
- *2 large onions, cut in wedges*
- *1 tablespoon hoi sin sauce*
- *1 tablespoon ground bean sauce*
- *¼ teaspoon five spice powder*
- *2 tablespoons dry sherry, optional*

Freeze lamb until firm enough to cut into paper-thin slices. Combine beaten egg with salt, sugar, garlic, soy sauce, cornflour and 1 tablespoon of peanut oil. Pour over lamb and mix well, cover and refrigerate for 2 hours.

Heat 1 tablespoon peanut oil in wok and fry onion wedges over high heat for 1 minute. Remove to a plate. Heat remaining oil, add lamb and stir-fry on high heat until brown. Add remaining ingredients mixed together and toss until well combined and heated through. Serve at once with rice.

Keep the vegetables crisp and crunchy and watch them disappear.

FIVE SPICE BEEF WITH VEGETABLES
Serves 4

- *750 g (1½ lb) rump steak*
- *½ teaspoon crushed garlic*
- *1 teaspoon finely grated fresh ginger*
- *½ teaspoon five spice powder*
- *1 cup broccoli sprigs*
- *1 large red capsicum*
- *2 teaspoons cornflour*
- *1 tablespoon dark soy sauce*
- *1 tablespoon dry sherry*
- *2 tablespoons peanut oil*
- *1 teaspoon oriental sesame oil*
- *3 spring onions, sliced diagonally*

Trim beef of any fat and freeze just until firm enough to cut into paper-thin slices. Combine garlic, ginger and five spice powder with beef.

Blanch broccoli in lightly salted boiling water for 1 minute, drain immediately. Slice capsicum in strips, discarding seeds. Combine cornflour, soy and sherry with ¼ cup cold water.

Heat peanut oil in wok and stir-fry capsicum for 30 seconds. Push aside and stir-fry meat, tossing until it changes colour. Stir sauce and cornflour mixture again and add to wok, stirring until it boils and thickens. Add broccoli, toss to combine all vegetables and meat with sauce and finally add sesame oil and spring onions and stir through. Serve at once with rice.

BEEF WITH PEANUT SAUCE
Serves 4

- *375 g (12 oz) rump steak*
- *3 tablespoons peanut oil*
- *½ teaspoon crushed garlic*
- *2 cups shredded Chinese cabbage*
- *3 spring onions, finely sliced*
- *½ cup beef stock*
- *1 tablespoon fish sauce*
- *3 teaspoons cornflour*
- *1 tablespoon smooth peanut butter*

Slice steak thinly. Heat peanut oil in wok, add meat and garlic and stir-fry over high heat for 2 minutes. Remove from wok and set aside. Add cabbage and spring onions and toss over high heat for 1 minute. Return meat, add stock and fish sauce and bring to boil. Push food to side of wok. Mix cornflour with 2 tablespoons cold water until smooth, stir into liquid until it boils and thickens. Stir in peanut butter. Serve with rice.

BEEF SALAD
Serves 4

- *500 g (1 lb) tender, lean grilling steak*
- *2 teaspoons Mild Green Curry Paste (see p. 72)*
- *1 clove garlic, crushed*
- *1 tablespoon chopped mint or coriander leaves*
- *freshly ground black pepper to taste*
- *1 tablespoon palm sugar or brown sugar*
- *2 teaspoons Maggi Seasoning (see Note)*
- *1 tablespoon lime juice*
- *2 teaspoons fish sauce*
- *½ teaspoon finely grated lemon rind*
- *8 small purple shallots, finely sliced or 4 sliced spring onions*
- *2 small seedless cucumbers, scored and sliced*
- *few sprigs fresh mint*

Rub steak with curry paste, leave 15 minutes. If you like barbecued flavour, cook beef over glowing coals, or grill until medium rare. Slice thinly when cool and firm.

Combine garlic, mint or coriander, pepper, palm sugar, Maggi Seasoning, lime juice, fish sauce and lemon rind. Place all ingredients in a bowl and toss lightly to distribute dressing.

Note   Maggi Seasoning is very similar in flavour to a Thai ingredient, Golden Mountain Sauce, and a lot more readily obtainable in Western supermarkets.

Buy American-style spareribs with tender meat and no fat for this delicious Asian version of 'finger-lickin' ribs'.

SPICY SPARERIBS
Serves 6 to 8

- 2 kg (4 lb) pork spareribs
- 2 teaspoons crushed garlic
- 1½ teaspoons salt
- freshly ground black pepper to taste
- 1 teaspoon five spice powder
- 2 tablespoons honey
- ¼ cup soy sauce
- 1 tablespoon oriental sesame oil

Separate ribs into groups of about 4 ribs each. Combine remaining ingredients and rub well over spareribs. Leave to marinate for 30 minutes.

Place in a roasting pan in preheated moderate oven, 180°C (350°F), and roast for 1 hour, turning ribs half way through cooking time and adding ½ cup water to pan at this stage. Baste with liquid in pan every 10 minutes until ribs are done. Serve hot with rice and bottled plum sauce.

Note The ribs may be cooked in a large frying pan. Brown lightly in 2 tablespoons peanut oil, then add ½ cup water and simmer, covered, until tender.

VEGETABLES AND SALADS

Most of the vegetables used in Asian dishes are familiar and readily available at the local greengrocer. But the spicy treatment gives them a lift.

SPICY FRIED BEANS
Serves 6

- 750 g (1½ lb) tender green beans
- 2 tablespoons oil
- 2 onions, finely chopped
- 1 teaspoon ground turmeric
- ½ teaspoon kalonji (nigella) seeds
- ½ teaspoon garam masala (see p. 73)
- salt to taste

String beans if necessary and cut into short lengths. Heat oil in a heavy pan and fry onion until soft and golden. Stir in turmeric, kalonji seeds and garam masala and fry for a few seconds. Add beans and salt, stirring to coat with spices. Reduce heat, add about ¼ cup water, cover and cook until beans are just tender.

Savoury Fried Potatoes
Serves 4 to 6

- *750 g (1½ lb) new potatoes, scrubbed and quartered*
- *3 tablespoons peanut oil*
- *1 teaspoon black mustard seeds*
- *2 onions, finely chopped*
- *1 teaspoon ground turmeric*
- *1 teaspoon ground cummin*
- *salt to taste*
- *fresh mint sprigs*

Boil or steam potatoes until tender. Heat oil in a heavy pan and fry mustard seeds until they pop. Add onions and sauté, stirring occasionally, until soft and golden. Stir in turmeric and cummin and fry for a minute. Add potatoes, sprinkle with salt and toss gently until ingredients are thoroughly mixed. Serve hot or cold, garnished with mint.

Vary the vegetables in this dish but whatever you do, don't overcook.

SPICED MIXED VEGETABLES
Serves 6

- *2 yellow squash, halved*
- *250 g (8 oz) butternut pumpkin, peeled and diced*
- *250 g (8 oz) green beans, topped, tailed and cut in half*
- *quarter of a cauliflower in florets*
- *half a small cabbage, sliced thickly*
- *3 tablespoons peanut oil*
- *½ teaspoon cummin seeds*
- *½ teaspoon black mustard seeds*
- *sprig of fresh curry leaves*
- *1 onion, finely chopped*
- *2 cloves garlic, chopped*
- *1 teaspoon finely grated fresh ginger*
- *1 teaspoon ground turmeric*
- *½ teaspoon garam masala (see p. 73)*
- *salt to taste*

Prepare vegetables and have ready.

In large saucepan heat oil and fry cummin and mustard seeds and curry leaves for 1 minute, stirring constantly. Add onion, garlic and ginger and fry until onion is soft. Stir in turmeric and garam masala.

Add carrots, beans and cauliflower. Cook, stirring, over

medium heat until vegetables are half cooked, then add cabbage and toss together until vegetables are tender but still crisp. Sprinkle with salt and mix well. Serve immediately with rice.

Who would have thought cold potatoes could be so delicious!

SPICY MASHED POTATOES
Serves 6

- *750 g (1½ lb) potatoes, peeled and sliced*
- *2 tablespoons melted butter*
- *hot milk*
- *¼ cup lemon juice*
- *salt to taste*
- *½ cup finely chopped fresh mint leaves*
- *2 tablespoons finely chopped spring onions*

Steam or boil potatoes until tender. Drain and mash while hot so they are quite smooth, adding hot milk to give a fluffy consistency. Stir in butter, lemon juice and salt. Mix in mint and spring onions. Pile into a bowl, garnish with sprigs of mint and serve at room temperature.

If snake beans (also called long beans) are not available, try this recipe with stringless beans.

STIR-FRIED SNAKE BEANS AND CASHEWS
Serves 4 to 6

- *500 g (1 lb) snake beans*
- *1 teaspoon cornflour*
- *½ cup Chicken Stock (see p. 1)*
- *1 tablespoon light soy sauce*
- *2 teaspoons oyster sauce*
- *2 tablespoons peanut oil*
- *2 teaspoons finely grated fresh ginger*
- *3 spring onions, chopped*
- *60 g (2 oz) deep-fried cashew nuts*

Trim beans, wash and dry. Cut into 5 cm (2 inch) lengths and set aside. Mix cornflour and 2 tablespoons cold water. Mix together Chicken Stock, soy and oyster sauces.

In a wok, heat oil and fry ginger for 10 seconds. Add beans and stir fry for 1 minute. Stir in sauce ingredients, cover and cook for 3 minutes. Stir in blended cornflour, cooking until it thickens sauce. Add spring onions and cashews and toss over high heat. Serve immediately.

Mixed Fruit Salad
Serves 6

- 6 cups mixed fresh fruit (e.g. slices of mango, pineapple, grapefruit and orange segments, seedless grapes)
  - ½ cup water chestnuts, sliced
  - 1 cup cooked, sliced chicken
  - 1 cup cooked, shelled prawns

Dressing
- ¼ cup sugar
- 2 tablespoons fish sauce
- 3 tablespoons lime juice
- 1 clove garlic, crushed

Garnish
- 2 tablespoons crisp-fried shallots
- 4 tablespoons roasted, salted peanuts, crushed
- washed lettuce leaves

Line serving plate with lettuce and cover with prepared fruits. Combine ingredients for dressing with ⅓ cup cold water and stir until sugar dissolves. Sprinkle 2 tablespoons over chicken and prawns and toss.

Place bowl with remaining dressing on platter so that it may be spooned over individual servings. Serve sprinkled with shallots and peanuts.

CHICKEN AND CABBAGE SALAD
Serves 6

- *half a white Chinese cabbage*
- *400 g (13 oz) chicken thigh fillets*
- *salt and pepper to taste*
- *1 medium onion, sliced thinly*
- *2 tablespoons sugar*
- *2 tablespoons fish sauce*
- *3 tablespoons lime juice*
- *1 tablespoon white wine vinegar*
- *½ cup chopped mint*
- *¼ cup chopped coriander*

Cut cabbage in halves lengthwise, wash in cold water and shake out all the water. Place cut surface down on wooden board, and with a sharp knife cut across into very thin slices. Cover and chill.

Gently simmer chicken fillets until tender with just enough water to cover, add salt and pepper to taste. Do not overcook. Allow to cool in liquid.

Sprinkle onion with ½ teaspoon salt and leave it for 30 minutes, then rinse under cold water, squeezing out juices. Add half the sugar and mix. Combine remaining sugar, fish sauce, lime juice and vinegar. Slice cooled chicken finely. Just before serving combine all the ingredients including mint and coriander and toss well.

ACCOMPANIMENTS AND USEFUL SPICE MIXTURES

A fresh chutney, not a cooked one, this has had the hot chilli taken out of it so that tender tastebuds won't be offended

FRESH MINT CHUTNEY
Makes about 1 cup

- 1 cup firmly packed mint leaves
- 6 spring onions, including green part, roughly chopped
- 1 clove garlic
- ½ teaspoon grated fresh ginger
- salt to taste
- 3 teaspoons sugar
- ½ teaspoon garam masala (see p. 73)
- ⅓ cup lime or lemon juice

Place all ingredients in blender or food processor with 2 tablespoons water and blend to a smooth purée, scraping down sides of bowl from time to time. Transfer to a small bowl, cover and chill. As well as being served with snacks and savouries, this chutney may be used as an accompaniment to curries, rice and breads.

This is one of those recipes which even conservative eaters take an instant liking to, with its combination of sweet, sour and salty flavours and fragrant seeds.

BANANAS IN SPICED YOGHURT
Serves 6

- 3 tablespoons desiccated coconut
- 1 cup plain yoghurt
- 2 tablespoons lemon juice
- 2 teaspoons sugar
- 1 teaspoon ghee
- 1 teaspoon cummin seeds
- 1 teaspoon kalonji (nigella) seeds
- salt to taste
- 3 large ripe bananas

Sprinkle 1 tablespoon hot water over coconut and mix until evenly moistened.

Combine yoghurt, lemon juice and sugar. Heat ghee in small saucepan and fry cummin and kalonji over gentle heat until they become fragrant. Add to yoghurt with coconut and stir. Add pinch of salt to accentuate flavours. Slice bananas and fold in. Serve as an accompaniment to curries.

A sweet-sour, very tangy fresh chutney made in a few minutes.

TAMARIND CHUTNEY
Makes about 1 cup

- 3 tablespoons dried tamarind pulp
- 1 tablespoon brown or raw sugar
- 1 teaspoon ground cummin
- ½ teaspoon ground fennel
- ½ teaspoon finely grated fresh ginger
- lime or lemon juice to taste
- salt to taste

Place tamarind pulp in a bowl and cover with 1 cup hot water. Leave to soak until water cools. Squeeze pulp until it dissolves. Strain through a nylon sieve, pushing all the pulp through, and adding a little more water if necessary. Discard fibres and seeds. Add remaining ingredients and stir until well mixed. Leftover chutney will keep in refrigerator for 1 or 2 days.

Make a smoother, richer version of this curry accompaniment by substituting sour cream for the yoghurt, or mixing the two.

CUCUMBERS IN YOGHURT
Serves 6

- 1 large seedless green cucumber
- salt to taste
- ¼ cup roughly chopped mint leaves
- 1 cup plain yoghurt
- lemon juice to taste

Wash cucumber, score skin and slice very thinly. Place in bowl, sprinkle with salt and chill for 1 hour. Pour off accumulated liquid, pressing to extract as much as possible. Mix mint with yoghurt, then stir into cucumbers. Add salt to taste, if necessary, and lemon juice. Chill until ready to serve.

Having a jar of Thai curry paste in the refrigerator is a wonderful convenience. Use sparingly to give good flavour without heat. Serve sambal oelek or Tabasco for seasoned chilli eaters to add.

MILD RED CURRY PASTE
Makes about ½ cup

- 2 large (mild) red chillies, optional
- 1 tablespoon paprika (see Note)
- 2 brown onions, chopped
- 1 tablespoon ground coriander
- 2 teaspoons ground cummin
- 1 teaspoon turmeric
- ½ teaspoon ground black pepper
- 2 tablespoons chopped fresh coriander stems and roots
- 1 teaspoon salt
- ½ teaspoon citric acid
- 1 stem lemon grass, finely sliced or 2 teaspoons chopped lemon rind
- 2 slices pickled galangal in brine
- 1 tablespoon chopped garlic
- 2 teaspoons dried shrimp paste

Discard stalks and seeds of chillies and place in food processor or electric blender with other ingredients. Blend until smooth paste forms, stopping frequently to push ingredients down

71

with spatula. You may need to add an extra tablespoon of water to assist with blending.

Note While paprika is not used in Thailand, I have added it to give the requisite red colour without using too many red chillies.

Without the tiny, fiercely hot green chillies used in Thailand this isn't truly authentic but is still fragrant and full of aroma without the pungent heat.

MILD GREEN CURRY PASTE
Makes about ½ cup

- *2 or 3 large, mild green chillies*
- *1 medium brown onion, chopped*
- *1 tablespoon chopped garlic*
- *1 cup firmly packed fresh coriander including roots*
- *thinly peeled rind of 1 lemon*
- *2 slices pickled galangal in brine*
- *2 teaspoons ground coriander*
- *1 teaspoon ground cummin*
- *¼ teaspoon ground black pepper*
- *1 teaspoon dried shrimp paste*
- *¼ cup lemon juice*
- *½ teaspoon citric acid*

Remove stems and seeds, chop chillies roughly and blend with all other ingredients in food processor or blender to a smooth purée. Store in clean, dry glass jar in refrigerator for 4 or 5 weeks and always use a clean, dry spoon to measure amount required. Or divide into portions, wrap and freeze.

Indian Spice Mixes

Garam Masala

- *2 tablespoons coriander seeds*
- *1 tablespoon cummin seeds*
- *2 teaspoons whole black peppercorns*
- *20 cardamom pods*
- *2 small cinnamon sticks*
- *10 whole cloves*
- *half a nutmeg*

In dry pan roast individual spices (except nutmeg) over low heat until fragrant, taking care not to let them burn. As each one is done turn onto a plate to cool. Peel cardamoms, using just the small dark seeds from within pods. Pound all spices together in mortar and pestle to very fine powder, or process in electric blender or coffee grinder. Finely grate nutmeg and mix in. Store in a tightly stoppered glass jar out of heat and light and it will retain its flavour for months.

Easy Garam Masala

- *2 tablespoons ground coriander*
- *1 tablespoon ground cummin*
- *2 teaspoons ground black pepper*
- *1 tablespoon ground cinnamon*
- *3 teaspoons ground cardamom*
- *1 teaspoon ground cloves*
- *2 teaspoons ground nutmeg*

Combine coriander, cummin and pepper and roast in dry pan until fragrant, stirring constantly and using low heat because powder will burn very easily. When they smell fragrant, turn onto a plate. Dry roast remaining spices on very low heat for a minute. Mix, cool completely and bottle airtight.

SNACKS AND SWEETS

POTATO AND PEA PASTRIES
Makes about 36

- *1 quantity of pastry (see p. 75) or 12 x 25 cm (10 inch) sheets spring roll pastry*
- *500 g (1 lb) potatoes, peeled and diced small*
- *1 teaspoon turmeric*
- *1 cup fresh or frozen peas*
- *1 small onion, finely chopped*
- *salt to taste*
- *1 teaspoon ground cummin*
- *½ teaspoon garam masala (see p. 73)*
- *2 tablespoons lime or lemon juice*
- *oil for deep frying*

Prepare pastry and set aside while preparing filling. Add turmeric to lightly salted water and boil potatoes until tender. Drain. If using fresh peas, cook until tender. If frozen, thaw only. Mix together potatoes, peas and onion with salt, cummin, garam masala and lime or lemon juice. Shape as for meat pastries (see p. 75), deep-fry a few at a time in hot oil and drain on paper towels. May be eaten warm or cold. Nice with Tamarind Chutney (see p. 70) for dipping.

Traditionally an afternoon tea snack in India, these small pastries are an ideal appetiser. A quick alternative to making pastry is to use spring roll wrappers, cut into strips and folded to form neat triangles. Serve hot or at room temperature, and, if liked, serve Mint Chutney (see p. 68) for dipping.

SAVOURY MEAT PASTRIES
Makes about 36

PASTRY
- 3 cups plain flour
- 1 teaspoon salt
- 1 tablespoon soft butter or ghee

FILLING
- 1 tablespoon oil or ghee
- 1 clove garlic, finely chopped
- ½ teaspoon finely chopped fresh ginger
- 2 medium onions, finely chopped
- 3 teaspoons mild curry powder
- salt to taste
- 1 tablespoon lime or lemon juice
- 375 g (12 oz) minced lamb or beef
- 1 medium potato, peeled and diced
- 1 teaspoon garam masala (see p. 73)
- 2 tablespoons chopped fresh mint
- oil for deep frying

PASTRY Sift flour with salt, rub in butter and add 1 cup lukewarm water. Mix well to form soft dough. Knead for 10 minutes—dough should be smooth and elastic. Wrap in plastic and leave to rest while preparing filling.

FILLING Heat oil in wok or saucepan. Fry garlic, ginger and onion, stirring, until onion softens. Stir in curry powder, salt and lime juice. Add minced meat and cook on high heat, stirring, until meat changes colour. Add potatoes and ½ cup hot water, stir, cover and simmer until meat and potatoes are tender and liquid absorbed, stirring from time to time towards end of cooking. Sprinkle with garam masala and chopped mint and leave to cool.

Shape dough into small balls and roll out on lightly floured surface into 20 cm (8 inch) rounds. Cut each round in thirds. Place tablespoon of filling on one side of part-circle, brush around edges with water. Fold over to enclose mixture and press edges together firmly to form triangle. When all are prepared, heat oil and deep-fry a few at a time until golden brown all over. Drain on paper towels.

Note If using spring roll pastry, cut each 25 cm (10 inch) square into 3 equal strips. Place filling at one end of strip and fold diagonally to make triangle. Continue folding until entire strip has been used. Moisten last flap with water and press to stick.

These are especially popular with children and surprisingly easy to make. Use frozen spring roll wrappers now available from most supermarkets and Asian stores. Thaw before using.

SPRING ROLLS
Makes 20

- 250 g (8 oz) pork fillet
- 250 g (8 oz) raw or cooked prawns
- 1 cup bean sprouts
- ½ small Chinese cabbage
- 2 tablespoons peanut oil
- 1 teaspoon crushed garlic
- 1 teaspoon finely grated ginger
- ½ cup finely chopped water chestnuts
- 8 spring onions, chopped
- 2 tablespoons light soy sauce
- salt to taste
- 3 teaspoons cornflour
- 1 teaspoon oriental sesame oil
- 1 packet 12.5 cm (5 inch) size frozen spring roll wrappers
- peanut oil for deep frying

Finely chop or mince pork. Shell and devein prawns then chop finely. Pinch straggly ends from bean sprouts. Finely shred ribs of cabbage to give 2 cups (save soft portion of leaves for salad). In wok heat half the oil and gently fry garlic and ginger for only a few seconds. Add pork, turn heat to high and cook, tossing, until it changes colour. Add prawns and fry 1 or 2 minutes longer. Add vegetables and toss until wilted, then add oyster sauce. Cook, tossing, for 1 minute. Mix cornflour with 1 tablespoon cold water. Push food to sides of wok and stir blended cornflour into liquid in centre of wok. Cook, stirring, until sauce boils and thickens. Transfer to large bowl and leave to cool.

Place 2 tablespoons of filling along centre of bottom edge of each spring roll wrapper and roll up, turning in ends as you go to enclose filling. Moisten top edge with water and press together to seal. Deep-fry spring rolls in hot oil, a few at a time, until golden. Drain on paper towels and serve warm.

SPICY POTATO RISSOLES
Serves 4

- 1 kg (2 lb) potatoes, peeled
- 1 teaspoon salt or to taste
- 1 tablespoon finely chopped mint leaves
- 3 spring onions, finely chopped
- ½ teaspoon ground cummin
- 1 egg, beaten
- breadcrumbs for coating
- oil for frying
- minced meat filling as prepared for Savoury Meat Pastries (see p. 75)

Boil potatoes, drain and mash until smooth. Mix in salt, mint, spring onions and cummin. Divide into 8 and shape each into a flat round. Put spoonful of filling in centre of each and surround with potato to form thick round patty. Dip in beaten egg, roll in breadcrumbs. Shallow-fry patties in hot oil until golden brown. Drain on paper towels, serve warm.

These little dumplings are both fried and steamed. Serve them with Chinese black vinegar (which is slightly sweet) or diluted malt vinegar mixed with a teaspoon of caster sugar, for dipping.

POT STICKERS
Makes 30

- 3 dried shiitake (Chinese) mushrooms
- 4 to 6 spring onions, finely chopped
- 250 g (8 oz) minced pork
- ¼ cup finely chopped water chestnuts
- 1 teaspoon finely grated fresh ginger
- 1 clove garlic, crushed
- ½ teaspoon salt or to taste
- 2 teaspoons light soy sauce
- 1 teaspoon oriental sesame oil
- 2 teaspoons cornflour
- ½ cup peanut oil, for cooking

DOUGH
- 2 cups plain flour
- 1 cup boiling water

Soak mushrooms in hot water for 30 minutes. Trim off and discard stems, chopping caps finely. Mix mushrooms, spring onions, pork, water chestnuts, ginger, garlic, salt, soy sauce and sesame oil. Blend cornflour with 2 tablespoons cold water and add to mixture, mixing by hand until thoroughly combined.

Dough Pour boiling water onto flour in a large bowl while stirring with chopsticks until combined. When mixture is cool enough to handle, knead on lightly floured surface until soft and smooth, dusting hands with flour if needed. Form dough into cylinder, then roll on a smooth surface until a long sausage—about 2.5 cm (1 inch) in diameter. Cut into 30 equal slices. Cover with damp cloth to keep moist.

Roll out each slice on a lightly floured board to form a circle 10 cm (4 inches) in diameter. Make overlapping pleats around one side of circle. Put a teaspoon of filling in pocket formed by pleats. Moisten edges and pinch together to seal. Cover dumplings with damp cloth, keeping them separate so they do not stick together.

Heat a large, heavy based frying pan over medium heat and add 4 tablespoons of oil to coat base and sides. Add half the dumplings, keeping pleats on top. Cook until golden underneath, loosening dumplings from base with spatula or frying slice to prevent them sticking. Boil 1 cup water and 2 tablespoons oil in separate pan and pour over dumplings, loosening any that are inclined to stick. (You can see how they got their name.) Bring to boil again, cover and cook for 5 minutes. Lower heat and cook for further 5 minutes. Uncover and cook until liquid evaporates, lifting dumplings to prevent sticking. They should be golden and crusty underneath. Repeat with remaining dumplings. Serve with chilli, soy or sweet vinegar dipping sauce.

An afternoon tea snack, but also an appetiser. The batter is usually made with chickpea flour, however to lessen its strong flavour and make the fritters more to children's tastes, this batter has been lightened with self-raising flour.

SAVOURY VEGETABLE FRITTERS
Makes about 36

- ½ cup chickpea flour (besan)
- 1 cup self-raising flour
- 1 teaspoon garam masala (see p. 73)
- salt to taste
- ½ teaspoon ground turmeric
- 1 teaspoon crushed garlic
- 4 cups raw vegetables of choice, cut into small dice
or thin slices—suggest eggplant, zucchini, onion, potato,
pumpkin, cauliflower, capsicum, spinach leaves

Sieve chickpea flour, self-raising flour, garam masala, salt, and turmeric into bowl. Add 1 cup water, stirring to make a thick batter. Add garlic and mix well. Rest batter for 30 minutes. Beat again before adding vegetables.

Drop mixture in teaspoons into deep hot oil and fry a few at a time until golden brown all over. (It is important not to fry too many at once as they will cause temperature of oil to drop, resulting in tough, oily fritters.) Drain on paper towels.

Just before serving, reheat oil and repeat frying process, cooking only 30 seconds in very hot oil. The secret to their crispness is the second frying. Drain on paper towels and serve warm with Tamarind Chutney (see p. 70) or Mint Chutney (see p. 68).

RICE BLANCMANGE
Serves 4

- *3 cups cold milk*
- *3 tablespoons ground rice*
- *¼ cup sugar*
- *½ teaspoon ground cardamom*
- *2 drops rose essence or 1 tablespoon rose water*
- *pink food colouring, optional*
- *2 tablespoons slivered blanched almonds*

Make a smooth cream by mixing a little milk with the ground rice. Heat remaining milk with sugar, stirring frequently until it boils. Turn off heat and stir in creamed ground rice. Return pan to heat and cook, stirring constantly for a few minutes, until mixture boils and thickens. Continue to cook for further 3 minutes. Sprinkle with cardamom, rose flavouring and a drop or two of food colouring, and stir until well mixed. Pour into individual dessert dishes and chill. Serve decorated with almonds.

Another Indian pudding the exotic flavourings of which turn simple semolina into something special.

SEMOLINA PUDDING
Serves 6

- ¾ cup sugar
- ½ cup milk
- ¼ teaspoon saffron threads
- 90 g (3 oz) ghee or unsalted butter
- ¾ cup fine semolina
- 2 tablespoons sultanas
- 2 tablespoons blanched slivered almonds or pistachios
- ½ teaspoon ground cardamom

In a saucepan, combine sugar and milk and 1 cup water. Bring to boil, stirring until sugar dissolves, then set aside. Toast saffron in a dry pan for 1 or 2 minutes without scorching, turn onto a saucer to cool and become crisp, then crush with back of a spoon and dissolve in a tablespoon of boiling water. Stir into milk mixture.

In a large saucepan melt ghee or butter, then fry semolina over low heat, stirring, until golden. Stir in milk syrup, sultanas, almonds or pistachios and cardamom. Stir over medium heat until mixture becomes thick and pulls away from sides of pan. Serve pudding warm, with cream if desired, or with Puris (see p. 20).

Alternatively, cooked mixture may be placed in a shallow buttered dish and left to cool, then cut into diamond shapes and decorated with extra almonds or pistachios.

An aromatic Indian dessert.

RICE PUDDING
Serves 4 to 6

- *½ cup short grain rice*
- *2 L milk (8 cups)*
- *8 cardamom pods, bruised*
- *1 cup sugar*
- *¼ cup slivered blanched almonds*
- *1 tablespoon rosewater or a few drops rose essence*
- *freshly grated nutmeg to taste*

Boil rice in water for 5 minutes. Drain well. Heat milk with cardamom pods in large saucepan and bring to boil. Stir in rice and simmer, stirring from time to time, for 1 hour or until rice is very soft and mixture quite thick. (It will be necessary to stir more frequently as mixture thickens, scraping any thickened milk from bottom and sides of pan.)

Add sugar and almonds and cook until a porridge consistency. Cool to lukewarm, remove cardamom pods and stir in rosewater. Serve warm or chilled with a little grated nutmeg sprinkled on top.

Glossary

You can find these ingredients in Asian stores but most of them are also sold in supermarkets.

Bamboo shoots Purchase in cans. Winter bamboo shoots are smaller and more tender.

Basmati rice A fragrant rice with fine, long grains. Requires washing. Leave 30 minutes in colander to drain and dry.

Cardamom Strongly fragrant seed pods of a plant of the ginger family, there are two kinds—large black pods or small green pods. Use the latter, bruised slightly to release fragrance. For ground cardamom, open pods and pound the small brown or black seeds inside with a mortar and pestle.

Chillies Handle with care as the volatile oils can cause much discomfort. Wear gloves when chopping. When adding this fiery ingredient to adult portions of a meal, substitute Tabasco sauce or sambal oelek. Small chillies are hotter than large ones and in recipes for family consumption, I suggest large chillies, sometimes known as banana chillies, for flavour without heat.

Cinnamon Most cinnamon is really cassia, which is not as delicate. True cinnamon quills have many layers of fine, pale brown bark and when ground are pale beige rather than brown.

Cloves The dried flower buds of a tropical tree. Can be overpowering, so don't use more than the stated amount.

Coconut milk Readily available but some brands of canned coconut milk are thick and rich, others very thin. Mix the former with at least an equal amount of water, use the latter undiluted.

Coriander Coriander seeds and fresh coriander are different in flavour and usage. Fresh coriander is often used in Thai, Indian and Chinese cooking.

Curry leaves (Murraya koenigii) Available as fresh curry leaves or you can grow the plant itself. Also sold dried.

Curry powder Buy reliable brands in tins or jars, in sizes you will use up within a few months so it doesn't outlast its effectiveness. Mild or medium strength if cooking for children.

Dried shrimp paste (Blachan) Powerful stuff, used in tiny quantities to bring out flavours in food. Keeps indefinitely. Don't let the children get a whiff of it, or they'll be convinced you are up to no good! Store in a screwtop jar to confine the smell.

Fish sauce A thin, salty sauce used in South-East Asian food much as soy sauce is used in Far Eastern food.

Five spice powder A fragrant mixture of ground star anise, fennel, cinnamon, cloves and Szechwan pepper.

Galangal An aromatic rhizome similar in size and appearance to ginger but with different flavour. Sold in large slices pickled in brine or as dried slices or powder. Also known as laos or lengkuas.

Garam Masala see page 73.

Ghee Clarified butter, sold in tins. Can be heated to a higher temperature without burning because it has no milk solids.

Ginger Fresh ginger root is sold at most greengrocers.

Ground bean sauce, bean sauce Made of soy beans, one is smooth while the other has large bits of fermented beans.

Kaffir lime leaves Essential in Thai cooking. Available fresh, frozen and dried.

Kalonji seeds (Nigella) Sometimes called black cummin though not a member of the cummin family. There is no substitute. Mostly from Indian shops.

Lemon grass Grows easily in Australia. Use the white or pale green tender portion of the stem which is tender enough to slice finely. Substitute 2 strips thinly peeled lemon rind for each stem of lemon grass.

Oyster sauce A thick, oyster flavoured sauce.

Palm sugar Obtained from various tropical palms, it has a distinct flavour but may be substituted by brown sugar.

Rice Vermicelli (or rice sticks, depending on the brand you buy) are fine, dried rice noodles usually popular with children.

Roti flour Also called Sharps, the term used by millers. Slightly granular, similar to Continental flour which may be substituted.

Saffron Try to get true saffron because there are imitations and nothing else has the same flavour. Expensive, but very little is needed. Keeps well if stored airtight. Best to buy the strands which are the dried stigmas of the autumn crocus, or tiny packets of powder. Distrust cheap saffron—there is no such thing.

Sesame oil Whenever sesame oil is called for, use oriental sesame oil made from roasted sesame which is dark in colour and very aromatic. Light coloured sesame oil (usually sold in health food stores) will not impart the same flavour.

Soy sauce There are many types—dark soy (thick, coloured with caramel); light soy (thin, saltier than dark); and Japanese soy (shoyu). For best results, use the specified kind.

Spring roll pastry Now available at supermarkets in the freezer section. These thin sheets of pliable pastry are most versatile and while they must be thawed to remove the number of sheets required, can be wrapped and re-frozen without ill effect. Available in various sizes, I find the 20 cm and 25 cm squares (8 inches and 10 inches) most useful.

Tamarind Gives acidity to many dishes. It is sold dried, puréed or instant. The dried pulp has the truest flavour.

Turmeric A tropical rhizome, it is most readily available as a yellow powder used to flavour and colour food.

INDEX

Accompaniments
bananas in spiced yoghurt 69
cucumbers in yoghurt 70
fresh mint chutney 68
tamarind chutney 70

Bananas in spiced yoghurt 69
Beans
snake, and cashews, stir-fried
65
spicy fried 61
Beef
five spice, with vegetables 57
salad 59
with peanut sauce 58
Bread
chapatis 19
parathas 20
Punjabi 18
puris 20
steamed Chinese buns 21
Buns, steamed Chinese 21

Chapatis 19
Chicken
and cabbage salad 67
and pineapple 41
and sweetcorn soup 7
barbequed or grilled 48
braised Mandarin 46
citrus, and pine nuts 47
curried, with cashews 50
drumsticks, red-cooked 42
Himalaya 40
in peanut sauce 49
rice, Hainan 13
simple steamed 44
spiced roast 39
steamed egg roll 37
stock 1
Thai, with snow peas 51
wings, honey soy 45
with almonds and broccoli 43
with rice noodles 17
Chutney
fresh mint 68
tamarind 70
Combination long soup 4
Cucumbers in yoghurt 70
Curry
chicken with cashews 50
fish, with tomato 23
omelette 38

paste, mild green 72
paste, mild red 71
prawn, with cream 29

Dessert
rice blancmange 82
rice pudding 84
semolina pudding 83
Dumplings, pot stickers 79

Egg roll, steamed 37
Eggs
in coconut milk sauce 33
in tamarind sauce 34
omelette curry 38
spicy scrambled 32
steamed egg roll 37
steamed, with mushrooms 36
stir-fried, with vegetables 35

Fish
cakes 30
curry with tomato 23
fried 25
in spiced yoghurt 28
piquant steamed 24
steamed, pudding 26
with coconut sauce 27
Fruit salad, mixed 66

Garam masala 73

Lamb
Kashmiri roast 53
kebabs 54
korma 52
Mongolian 56
with vegetables, stir-fried 55
Lentils
and rice, savoury 14
mulligatawny 8
Long soup, combination 4

Marinades 39, 40, 45, 53, 54, 55,
56, 60
Meat
mixed, and vegetable soup 5
savoury, pastries 75
Meatballs with soup 2

Noodles
egg, salad 16
rice, crispy 15
rice, with chicken 17

Omelette curry 38

Parathas 20
Pastry 76
    egg roll wrappers 38
Pea and potato pastries 74
Pork
    pot stickers 79
    spicy spareribs 60
Pot stickers 79
Potatoes
    and pea pastries 74
    savoury fried 62
    spicy mashed 64
    spicy rissoles 78
Prawn
    cakes 30
    curry with cream 29
    stir-fried, with vegetables and
        oyster sauce 31
Pumpkin and coconut soup, Thai
    6
Puris 20

Rice
    and lentils, savoury 14
    blancmange 82
    Hainan chicken 13
    pudding 84
    saffron 11
    simple fried 10
    spiced Parsi 12
    steamed white 10

Salad
    beef 59
    chicken and cabbage 67
    dressing 59, 66, 67
    egg noodle 16
    mixed fruit 66
Sauce
    citrus 47
    coconut 27
    coconut milk 33
    dipping 14, 30, 42
    garlic, chilli and fish sauce 36
    peanut 49, 58

pineapple 41
    tamarind 34
Semolina pudding 83
Short soup 3
Snacks
    pot stickers 79
    potato and pea pastries 74
    savoury meat pastries 75
    savoury vegetable fritters 81
    spicy potato rissoles 78
    spring rolls 77
Soup
    chicken and sweet corn 7
    chicken stock 1
    combination long 4
    lentil mulligatawny 8
    mixed meat and vegetable 5
    short 3
    Thai pumpkin and coconut 6
    with meatballs 2
Spice mixtures
    garam masala 73
    mild green curry paste 72
    mild red curry paste 71
Spring rolls 77

Tamarind chutney 70

Vegetables
    and mixed meat soup 5
    and oyster sauce, with stir-fried
        prawns 31
    lentil mulligatawny 8
    potato and pea pastries 74
    pumpkin and coconut soup,
        Thai 6
    rice and lentils, savoury 14
    savoury fried potatoes 62
    savoury, fritters 81
    spiced mixed 63
    spicy fried beans 61
    spicy mashed potatoes 64
    stir-fried snake beans and
        cashews 65
    with eggs, stir-fried 35
    with five spice beef 57
    with lamb, stir-fried 55